NO PLACE TO CRY

THE HURT AND HEALING OF SEXUAL ABUSE

Doris VanStone and Erwin W. Lutzer

MOODY PRESS
CHICAGO

ISBN: 0-8024-2272-2

1 3 5 7 9 10 8 6 4 2

Printed in the United States of America

To my grandchildren:
Whitney, Erica, Lynsey, Derek, Natalie, Lorien

Precious gifts, loved of God,
who gave me the privilege of being called
"Grandmother"

Contents

Foreword

Are you overwhelmed by pain? The pain of incest, abuse, rejection, a dysfunctional family . . . ?

When Jeremiah looked at the brokenness of his people, he cried out in dismay, "Is there no balm in Gilead? Is there no physician there? Why then has not the [healing] of the daughter of my people been restored?" (8:22).

Jeremiah knew that healing was possible. God's name is Jehovah Rapha, which means the God who heals, and God has a balm, a healing salve—His Word. That's why Jeremiah was dismayed. He knew that there was no wound or hurt so great, so horrible, so seemingly destructive that our sovereign God could not heal it. He is God, the God of all flesh, and nothing is too hard for Him.

If there is any story that will illustrate this truth, you will find it within the covers of *No Place to Cry.*

Maybe you read Dorie's first book, *Dorie: The Girl Nobody Loved*, and saw God's power to heal but said in your heart, "She was never sexually violated, so healing was possible for her, but . . . "

There are no "buts," beloved reader. There is no wound God cannot heal! You will see this truth confirmed over and over again as you read for the first time the part of

Dorie's story that she has never told before except to a few intimate friends.

It is a hard story to tell. But for Jesus and for the sake of His people Dorie is willing to let you look into the dark, musty closet of her past so that you might see how the Light of the World came into that closet, bringing with Him the sweet aroma of His sovereign love.

Dorie is living testimony of God's power to heal the deepest of hurts, and it is my privilege to hug her every time she comes home to me and to our Precept Family.

Read her book prayerfully, and walk with God in child-like faith even as Dorie did and does—and you'll find yourself being healed because there *is* a balm in Gilead and a great Physician there.

KAY ARTHUR

Acknowledgments

I want to give a special word of thanks to the many hundreds of people who have written to me during the last several years. Many of your letters have found their way into this book. Though I was unable to contact each of you to let you know I used your comments, be assured that the effects of your insights and encouragement will be multiplied one hundredfold.

I also want to thank my dear friend Dr. Erwin Lutzer, the pastor of Moody Church, for writing the manuscript that so accurately reflects my experiences and thoughts. We spent many hours together in discussion, and I rejoice in the great ministry that this new book will have.

Also I am grateful for my dear friend Ray Martin, who gave me some "days away" to get my thoughts together for this book.

And thank you to dear Sandy Burdick, who took a risk and with gentle probing found the child inside the armor.

Thank you for your help. My prayer is that the Lord will use this book to His glory.

Dear Dorie:

Dorie, my problem is that I cannot believe that God loves me. I know in my head that He does, but I don't know it on a deeper level. I can't accept it, because I'm afraid that if I did He would reject me. It's an emotional block, not a reasonable one. Everything would be OK if I just knew that Jesus loved me, if I knew that He cared and would carry me through my circumstances. Then I could survive the struggles and the pain of my past. All I really need is love. You broke through my defenses, although I fought very hard. I said to myself, "I will not cry! This is baloney! It's all just emotion that will fade away, and I won't let it touch me!" But I knew it wasn't baloney that if I let down my defenses and let the tears come and accept God's love, there would be healing.

Love,
T.

Introduction

On Saturday, June 29, 1985, at about 1:30 in the afternoon an ambulance sped down Randolph Street. Lloyd and I were in Topeka, Kansas, visiting our son, Burney, and his wife. I watched the ambulance from their house.

I glanced up into the eyes of our daughter-in-law, Diana. "I hope it's not for Lloyd," I said, only half seriously.

"I'm sure it's not," she answered.

My husband had come to love jogging during the past several years. He was in good shape and enjoyed the relaxation and exercise. I was not worried, for he was not expected back for another half hour.

Earlier, he had come into the kitchen in his jogging shorts. "Sweetie, I'll be back in a little while, and then we'll go out to eat."

He bent over and kissed me. I hugged him once—then twice. After he walked out of the house, I went to the door.

"Have a good run!" I shouted.

He turned back to look at me and pointed his index finger to the sky. "I will, honey!" he called back.

Now we were waiting. An hour passed, and he did not return.

I decided to walk to the park and look for him. Surely he would be there, perhaps relaxing in the sun. But he was nowhere to be seen. Even then, I would not allow myself to consider what might have happened.

When I returned, we discussed what to do next. Though no one mentioned it, we could not get that ambulance out of our minds.

We hopped into the car and drove along the street still expecting to see him. Perhaps he had made a wrong turn or taken a walk along a side street.

We returned home bewildered. I asked Diana to phone the nearby hospital. As she listened to the voice at the other end, her face turned white and her hand shook. "Dorie, they brought in an unidentified man—they think he was a runner—we are to come immediately."

We drove to the hospital in silence. Surely, it would not be Lloyd. *It can't be, Lord. No, it can't be.*

When we arrived, a man wearing a hospital uniform met us. "You stay here," he told me. "Let your son come with me."

We waited for what seemed an eternity. Then Burney returned, his hands outstretched. Before he spoke I knew what had happened. "Mother, he's gone."

"No, it can't be!"

"Yes, Mom, he's home free."

Diana joined us as we wept in one another's arms. I felt as if I were dreaming. Lloyd had said he'd be home in time for us to go get something to eat. *He could not have died that quickly,* I said to myself.

After gaining his composure, Burney said, "You know, before I walked out of that room, I kissed him and said, 'O Lord, I have to be a different man when I walk out of here.'" Then he added, "Mom, I want to be like him!"

"There is only one way that you can be like him," I said. "Love the Lord your God with all your heart, soul, and mind."

"Soldier, are you ready?" Burney asked, wondering if I was prepared to walk into the room where my dear husband lay.

"I'm ready."

I walked silently into the room and saw my Prince Charming, lying in the stillness of death. I kissed him and wept. For one fleeting moment I thought, *If only I had told him good-bye.* Then I remembered, *No, I didn't have to tell him good-bye. Everything in our lives was up-to-date—for thirty-six years we had repeatedly said to each other, "I love you."*

The doctor told us that someone had actually seen Lloyd fall. He died instantly, possibly before his body hit the ground. He died, the doctor said, in mid-step.

"Do you realize what you are telling me?" I asked. "Lloyd ran straight into heaven!"

The doctor patted my shoulder and replied, "Uh huh," as if to say, "I've seen this before when they're in shock."

But to this day I like to think that God said to Lloyd, "Soldier, it's time to come home!"

Then I imagine Lloyd's saying, "Lord, but Dorie—"

"Don't worry. I will take care of her. You come on home."

The Pain

Every woman grieves the loss of her husband. But in my case the loss was especially intense for one reason: Lloyd was the first person in all the world ever to truly love me.

We met while attending St. Paul Bible College in September of 1946. The moment I saw him, I admired the tall, handsome Texan. I never dreamed I would have the good fortune of having him as my husband. *Of course he'd reject me if he knew me*, I reasoned.

Those who have endured physical and sexual abuse will understand that I felt dirty, ashamed, and unworthy of human love. No matter how much I tried to be like everyone else on the outside, I knew I was different on the inside. And I thought that everyone else could see inside me.

If people could have looked inside, what would they have seen?

I had been conceived out of wedlock, and my conception forced my parents into an early marriage. I was hated by my mother and abused in an orphanage and two foster homes. My mother completely rejected me. I experienced ridicule and repudiation. I was sexually molested. And I was eventually disowned by my father.

My earliest memories date back to a lonely apartment in Oakland, California, where as a child I would wait in darkness for my mother to come home. My mother gave me the responsibility of taking care of my younger sister, Marie. When Mother would arrive home, she would give Marie a hug. I was always pushed aside like an unwanted dog.

I was only six, but I knew deep pain. We often went to bed hungry. But the pain of an empty stomach was more bearable than the emotional hurt of rejection and hatred. I was never held, touched, or cuddled. I knew I was different, ugly, and a burden to my mother.

Often she would bring male companions home with her. Then she would dress my younger sister, and all of them would go out together. To make sure no one would discover that a child had been left behind alone, she would take the wall bed down, stuff me inside it, and then put it up again. There I would cry, gasping for air until I fell asleep.

Occasionally people have asked how I can remember events dating back to age six. All I can answer is that when the pain is deep, you *do* remember. My memories are still vivid.

When I was seven, my mother took Marie and me to an orphanage, dropping us off like a package at the door. She visited us just twice in seven years, bringing only a gift for Marie—none for me. Years later when Lloyd and I visited the orphanage, I discovered to my surprise that it was only ten blocks from the apartment in which my sister and I had lived with our mother. At the time it seemed a world away.

In the orphanage I took out my anger on the other children. I deservedly earned a bad reputation and was beaten (usually just before bedtime) every evening for seven years.

But when I was thirteen, some Christian students came to tell us about Jesus Christ. As they were leaving one of them said, "Children, even if you forget everything else we have told you, remember—*God loves you.*"

Sitting on a folding chair in the parlor, I prayed for the first time in my life. I told God that if He loved me and wanted me, He could have me. On that special day I became a Christian, and I knew I was received by God. At last, I had a Friend—a Friend forever.

Little did I realize that for me life outside the orphanage would be far worse than it was within its walls. I was shunted to four foster homes. In two, I was physically, mentally, and sexually abused. Yet the God who was with me during my closing days in the orphanage stood with me.

Much later in my life I was able to locate my father. We formed a friendship, and I lived with him and his wife for one and a half years. But when I told him that I was going to be a missionary, he rejected me—I was not even allowed inside his house though I had made a special trip to tell him about my decision. When he died, the record stated that he had no children. He rejected me to the very end.

With the scars of all of those hurtful experiences lodged in my heart, I often wondered whether God would ever use me or whether *anyone* would love me. I kept my past largely to myself, for I soon discovered that most people are too preoccupied with their own lives to bear someone else's burdens. I also didn't trust many people. I feared that if people found out about my past, I would only be rejected again and *again*.

God had been with me through those dark childhood days of physical and spiritual hurt. But I craved the love of at least one human being, one person who could accept me as I was, one person who would love me despite my past.

Lloyd was that person.

To me it was a miracle of God's grace that Lloyd and I began to date. One day we walked past a jewelry store. "Let's stop and look at rings. I want to get one for you," he blurted without warning. Almost in shock I looked up, and he whispered those three short words I had longed for so deeply: "I love you!" Then he kissed me.

Think of it!

He loved me though I had been hated by my family; he loved me though I was ugly. *He loved me though I had been robbed of my virginity by the cruel actions of evil men.* I had always thought of myself as "damaged goods." And not merely damaged but rejected. Hated. But here was a man prepared to spend the rest of his life with me. He knew my past, and it did not matter.

The Funeral

Lloyd's funeral was on July 2, 1985. My dear friend Rev. Erwin Lutzer, the pastor of Moody Church in Chicago, flew to Kansas City to speak at the funeral. He brought a message of the faithfulness of God and His love for His children. He quoted someone as saying, "God is too good to do anything bad and too wise to make a mistake."

When I left the cemetery, the fact that I was a brand-new widow hit me. The only man I had ever loved—the only man who had ever really loved me—was gone. I was happy for him, for I knew that he was with Jesus. But I knew that many nights I would have to cry myself to sleep in loneliness because I would never feel his tender touch again.

The pain of losing Lloyd was just as deep as the hurts of my childhood—in some ways deeper. I began the early years of my life knowing only the love of God; it seemed now that I shall end my life the same way. But now I have hundreds of

Christian friends, and some are even closer to me than a brother or a sister. Kay and Jack Arthur of Precept Ministries in Chattanooga have welcomed me into their family. I live on their campus, share their joy and friendship, and am privileged to be a part of their ministry. How I love my Precept family!

I have two precious children and six grandchildren. Yet, having known the joys and intimacies of marriage, I have had to adjust to the fact that life without Lloyd will never be the same. But with God how can I be disheartened? Today I still hear the words He spoke to me when I lived in the orphanage in Oakland, when I was mercilessly beaten in my foster homes, and when I was sexually molested: "Dorie, I will be with you. I will be all you ever need."

The apostle Paul wrote that God "comforts us in all our affliction so that we may be able to comfort those who are in any affliction with the comfort with which we ourselves are comforted by God" (2 Corinthians 1:4).

As I speak at conferences around the country, I have found that hurting people quickly identify with me because I have walked the path they are traveling. I know the path of private pain, the path of loneliness and of despair. But I also know the path of healing and grace. This book is an invitation for you to walk with me. Come to my counseling room, and listen to the hurts of those who feel pain so deeply that they can barely speak of it. Hear stories of whippings, sexual molestation, and verbal abuse. But please do not stop there. Stay long enough also to hear the victories, reconciliations, and healings.

Those who have read *Dorie: The Girl Nobody Loved* will find that this book takes them a step further. This book adds details to that story. Not only was I abused physically and verbally but also sexually. When the first book was written, I did not yet feel comfortable revealing the full extent of the mistreatment I experienced. Sexual abuse is difficult for victims to talk about—no one wants to recall such painful events. And until recent years victims were expected to keep such secrets *secret*. But I can no longer be silent. This account also provides more detailed principles on how to let God heal the hurts. Most important, it tells of God's healing grace in the midst of sexual abuse.

Almost every time I speak I am sought out by women who suffer from sexual abuse. One-sixth of the female population today has been abused. As the influence of pornography and moral decay increases in our society, the rate of sexual abuse will also rise. One estimate says that one out of four baby girls born this year will be sexually abused, usually by a member of the immediate family, a relative, or a friend.

Boys are also abused, often by homosexuals who develop a craving for "younger talent," as it is called in the world of perversion. Some are abused in different ways by their parents or peers.

I have been gratified that God has used my previous book to minister to so many people. One woman wrote, "Your book was part of the healing process in my life. As I read page after page I saw so much of my own life . . . it really hurt, but it was a *clean* hurt."

I was encouraged by a letter I received from a man in the Philippines. He had read *Dorie* to the students at his academy. He acknowledged that mine was a sad story but then added that he began to see the bright spots in it:

> I thanked God for your mother, who in spite of her hatred for you, allowed you to live. I thanked God for your father who, by turning his back on you, threw you unto the mercy and love of God. I thanked God for the love of your husband, Lloyd, who showed you what human love could be like. And I thank God for all the cruel people who came into your life, for they made you into the woman you are today.

I wept as I read that letter. I experienced childhood trauma for a reason. The scars are still there, but they don't hurt as they once did. There is hope.

Some people think that saying that Christ is the answer to emotional pain is too simplistic. In one of my meetings a distinguished gentleman sat in the front row, listening intently to every word. I suspected that he was there to critically evaluate my talk on "Healing Hurts." I was right.

"Simplistic," he said after the meeting. Then he added, "I'm a practicing psychiatrist." At that I wanted to leave, fearing the coming lecture. But he wouldn't let me go. "I'm also a Christian," he said. "And I have been letting the pressure of my peers get to me. So recently I started giving patients a copy of your book, along with a copy of the Bible." I was relieved to hear that he was encouraging me. He had concluded that saying Christ is the answer sounds simple but is also correct—the Lord came to heal the broken-hearted and to set at liberty those who are bruised.

Thus this is a book of hope. We do not have to work though our problems alone. Christ, the wonderful Counselor, stands with us to help us through the process. He is the answer for this hurting world.

I am not a professional counselor. But I do have two qualities that have helped others with backgrounds similar to mine. First of all, I can identify with emotional aches and pains. I have learned to listen and to believe the stories I hear, for I have walked in your shoes. Second, I have a firm faith in the power of Christ, who is able to heal the hurts of the past.

This book is about triumph, for Christ is the answer! My earnest prayer is that thousands will discover that God allows us to be wounded only that He might heal us. I want to tell this bruised world that there is a Savior who can make us each whole.

Dear Dorie:

When you shared your life, you connected . . . you touched the person deep inside where the pain is so intense.

My sisters and I were molested by our father. God has removed the shame that kept me from talking about my past. For so long I was hurting, locked up within myself, but the dark areas needed to be exposed.

My father was a pastor. Am I to be impressed when a person is a Sunday school teacher, a missionary, or in any job held for God? I say look at their children, if you find the child within. Sometimes there is a dark evil and loneliness in these families.

We need to be held up to the light, just like a broken pot, to see if there is a fault or not. I've given God my broken pot that I had tried to make look perfect. Now that it has been exposed to God's light, He can shine His love through me. I am His pot—the broken pot that no one would want to love and be proud of. One broken pot knows another broken pot. He heals the broken pots.

Because of Jesus,
M.

1
No Place to Cry

Someone has rightly observed that the trouble abused children face is that they have no place to cry their eyes out. Think of what it must be like to have to bear the dark secret of abuse alone. To tell someone in authority is to risk punishment or disbelief.

To my dismay I have learned that sexual abuse can take place in Christian homes—even in the homes of Christian leaders. This hidden sin happens behind the closed doors of some of our most respected families. It happens everywhere.

Those dark secrets are what cause the soul to become bitter, unloving, and woefully sad. They are the cause of many neuroses, and they also lead to withdrawal from society or even the contemplation of suicide.

The part of our souls that we keep from one another (and perhaps also from God) becomes the seat of our troubles. Many people could be greatly helped if they could find a listening ear and a sympathetic heart.

For years I concealed a secret that I determined only God and my husband would know about. I thought they were the only ones I could trust. I thought people would not believe me if I told them that I had been sexually abused.

But now I tell my story because I have met hundreds of women who can identify with my suffering.

My sister and I left the orphanage when I was thirteen years old. We were taken to a foster home run by a woman we called "Granny." I attended junior high school, and Marie went to an elementary school nearby.

Granny began to intimidate us the day of our arrival. "If you don't mind me, you'll get *this*," she warned as she slapped my face with her bare hand, using me as an example. The blows stung, but I tried not to cry.

There was, however, something far worse than the beatings I endured in Granny's home. One evening when I was sleeping, her husband came into my room, woke me, and told me to take off my clothes. Then without further explanation, he forced me to participate in sexual acts to satisfy his perverted whims and desires.

That was the first of many such experiences. *How I hated the very sight of the man!* He was tall, strong, and heavyset. There was nothing I could do to stop him from violating my body. He warned me that if I ever told anyone he would kill me, and I believed him. After almost every one of those traumatic encounters, he would lock me into a closet until I stopped crying. If I cracked open the door and he was still around, he would abuse me again. One time I sobbed with such intensity and anger that I pushed my hands right through my pockets.

The only thing that sustained me during those painful days was the knowledge that God was with me. Back in the orphanage, a Christian matron by the name of Irma Freman had given me a copy of the New Testament. Each day I would read a few verses, trying to memorize them as well as I could. "Lord, You promised to be with me all the time," I would say. "All I have is You."

After about four months with Granny, Marie and I were taken to a home for girls who were wards of the state. There we had a welcome respite from the cruelty of the past few months. Unfortunately, our stay was short-lived. We were told that we would be transferred into a private home. We looked forward to this, thinking we might actually find someone who loved us. But that was not to be.

Oh No, Not Again

When the doorbell at the Girls' Home rang, I was stunned. There stood Granny, looking as angry as ever. "We've come to take you to a family that lives in San Francisco," she said, pointing at the social worker who was with her.

Granny, we discovered, knew our mother. We never quite understood the connection, but we were told that she was there on our mother's behalf. My sister was taken to live with a family who really wanted her. I was taken to live with a family that knew my mother.

Life in the Makin home was as bad as, if not worse than, what I experienced at Granny's. Mr. Makin was a short, stocky man with a heavy chest. He reminded me of a gorilla. Mrs. Makin looked stern with her gray hair parted down the middle. Mrs. Makin permitted me to take only one bath a month and to wash my hair every eight weeks. Over the door she kept a calendar indicating the day she would draw the water into the tub. I would have to strip in front of her, and when I was wet, she would beat me with a leather strap. I can still feel the sting.

Often I was beaten just before leaving for school, so I had to begin the five-mile walk with a bloody nose or black eye. I would use the restroom in a service station before I arrived so that I could attempt to camouflage my hurts. I'm convinced now that my teachers and other adults must have seen that I was being abused. But they pretended not to notice. If they had asked questions, they would have become responsible. Apparently no one wanted to get involved.

My hair became matted, and I developed head lice. So my hair was shaved off. To hide my embarrassment, I went to school with my head wrapped in a towel. The other children would pull it off and laugh, calling me cruel names.

Dirt encased itself around my wrists and ankles. When I walked into the classroom, I'd hear the other students say, "There's Stinky!" as they turned their backs toward me.

I looked forward to that long walk to and from school. I used the time to talk to God. Sometimes after school I would crawl into boxes in an alley or crouch behind trash cans, seeking some sort of refuge. I sought a place to pray and cry my eyes out.

The beatings I had come to expect at Granny's were repeated at the Makins. They beat me mercilessly. Once again, I found myself running outside to hide under a step or in an alley, always looking for a place to cry.

My rollaway bed was in the hallway that led from the dining hall to the Makins' bedroom. Frequently strange men walked past my couch, shuffling their way into the bedroom. I prayed that they would not touch me.

One day Mrs. Makin said to one of the men, "Go ahead, take her. I'll stay in the other room." The man overpowered me. He tore my clothes and forced me to participate in his sexual acts. Once again, I found myself screaming, begging, pleading that I might not have to become a part of these perversions. But no one listened to my cries. No one came to help.

Soon other men would come to the house looking for "the little girl." The houses in San Francisco are built so close to one another that there is only room for a small alley between them. Sometimes when I heard the men coming I would run through the alley and hide under a step or run to the other side of the block. I still recall hiding one evening and overhearing the men saying to one another, "Where is she? Where could she have gone?"

I had scraped my knee as I crouched in the small crevice, waiting for the men to leave. Rotting garbage must have been near me because I vividly recall thinking that it smelled like dead rats. Amid my tears I sobbed, "If only I had a mother, this would not be happening to me!" Then a light seemed to engulf me, and I felt a sense of peace. I heard the men say, "She's not here." They left. That time God protected me.

But there were times when God did not protect me. I prayed earnestly for deliverance, calling to the Lord for help and protection, but still I was sexually abused by evil men. Once I threw a cup of hot coffee on one of my attackers but was beaten and abused all the more severely.

No one had to tell me that what was happening was perverted and filthy. It is impossible to exaggerate the sense of shame and revulsion that those acts brought to my soul. For a long time I would run from anyone who wanted to touch me, even if it was an innocent touch.

God did not shield me from the violations of my body, yet I still clung to Him, believing that He would be with me. He gave me the grace to bear my trials. That's why I have never been bitter or angry with my heavenly Father. It was He who chose me to belong to Him; He led those students to the orphanage to tell me about God's love. Regardless of the heartaches I have endured on earth, I know that this present suffering cannot be compared with the glory that will be revealed in us. God has reserved a place for me in heaven, so that I may be with Him forever. Eternity is a long time. Someday I shall speak to my Savior, who stood with me when no one else did. Maybe He will tell me why I had to endure all those tears. And maybe He will point to some people and say, "Dorie, these are here because you told them about My grace and power." Just a word from my Savior will make up for the past.

I believe God is sovereign; He knew the first day of my life, and He knows the last, as well as all the days in between.

Nothing can happen to me without first passing through His fingers of love. He knew that some day that dirty little girl would stand before thousands of people and tell them that God is faithful—that there is nothing in their lives too big for God to handle.

People have told me, "Dorie, you've survived because you had such strong faith." That's not true. I survived because there was no one else to run to except the Lord. I had absolutely no one else. I sometimes questioned God, but I never hated Him.

Do I have scars? Of course. But there is something beautiful about a scar. It means that you have been healed —that you are on the mend. All over the country I meet people who have been cut open emotionally, and many of them still have open wounds. Sometimes I meet people who are holding onto their bitterness; they keep reliving the painful events of the past. They are, in effect, peeling off the scabs to see whether healing has occurred—or sometimes to prove that it hasn't.

The process of healing is like major surgery. After the operation, the wound is painful and tender, but if the stitches do their job, healing occurs. Slowly the flesh begins to grow together, and the area becomes whole again. Eventually you can be hit where the scars are without feeling it.

Today I tell people, "Don't blame God for what happens to little children!" It is true that terrible things happen within the context of His permissive will and that He could prevent them. But He does not *do* the evil, and He has good reasons for allowing those things to happen.

Job did not curse God even though he lost his children, possessions, and health. His wife advised, "Curse God and die." But he called her foolish, asking, "Shall we indeed accept good from God and not accept adversity?" (2:10). Thus Job did not sin with his lips or charge God foolishly.

Also, I have to remind my listeners, "Don't believe the psychiatrists who state that experiences of abuse will ruin you for the rest of your life and that you will never be normal." Unfortunately, many people have believed the lie that past abuse will ruin all your chances for happiness. Not so. When Christ promised that our joy would be full, I believe He meant it for all Christians, regardless of their backgrounds. He is indeed able to heal the broken-hearted. For example, I had the good fortune to be married to an understanding husband who loved me despite my abuse. He was tender and compassionate, and through his love the sexual relationship became beautiful and fulfilling. That is proof of what God is able to do.

The Value of Tears

I know what it is like to try to find a place to cry my eyes out. Often during those difficult years I would specifically look for a place to cry—a closet, a vacant lot, or an alley. If all the tears I have shed could be collected, I'm quite sure they would fill a bucket or two. Tears are a necessary part of handling grief.

In two incidents recorded in the New Testament, Jesus wept. He stood at the grave of Lazarus, and He looked compassionately over the city of Jerusalem—in those instances our Lord participated in the grief of mortals. His tears give ours legitimacy.

I've often pondered the words of David, who himself shed many tears because of the oppression of wicked men. "My foes have trampled upon me all day long," he writes. "For they are many who fight proudly against me" (Psalm 56:2). He continues, "All day long they distort my words; all their thoughts are against me for evil. They attack, they lurk, they watch my steps, as they have waited to take my life" (vv. 5-6).

Was God taking note of the mistreatment David received at the hands of his enemies? Notice what follows: "Thou hast taken account of my wanderings; put my tears in

Thy bottle; are they not in Thy book?" (v. 8). David believed his tears were put in a bottle; they were recorded in God's special book. God did that for David, and I like to think that He has done the same for me. My tears were noticed by God, collected as a symbol of my suffering and His special care. I have not cried in vain. Those tears, though long since dried, have not escaped the attention of God. My friend, you can safely cry in God's presence. Someday He will wipe the tears from your eyes, but until that time He collects them as precious perfume in His sight.

A young lady wrote, "Dear Dorie, thank you for letting me cry. I've prayed that the Lord would send me someone who knew what my heart felt. I've got good friends, but I needed someone to touch me who knew my pain. Now I can go on, knowing that someone who knows touched me."

Let us as the Body of Christ allow people the privilege of crying. Some women were never allowed to be children when they were growing up. As far back as they can remember they have borne hurts that are even too much for adults. The little girls inside still need to come out. Let us permit them to cry.

My heart still breaks for the thousands of children out there who are being abused, either physically or sexually (or both), who do not know Christ as their Savior. They have to withstand the trauma alone, and they have nowhere to turn. To them God may seem cold, impersonal, and cruel. Some lash out in anger against the Almighty and against the people who have mistreated them. Even after they grow up and become integrated into society, they live alone emotionally. They never really feel as if they belong to anyone. No one helps them carry their trauma; no one makes their burden lighter. The family they marry into is often just as cruel as the one that reared them.

Christ already knows our dark secrets. We share our inmost thoughts, and He lends His listening ear. The same Christ who forgave my sins and enabled me to come to grips with my troubled past is available to you. His death on the cross was a sacrifice for sinners so that we all can be welcomed into His family forever. We must, however, receive Him as our own. In the orphanage in Oakland I put my faith in Him and received both His companionship and the gift of eternal life. If you have not already done that, don't read any further. You have business with God.

The first step in experiencing the healing of the past is to choose to deal with those dark secrets. Bring them to God. He knows about them already, of course; indeed, He knows every detail of our history. By taking up the matter with our heavenly Father, we have the advantage of talking with someone who already knows the details if words fail us. "And in the same way the Spirit also helps our weakness; for we do not know how to pray as we should, but the Spirit Himself intercedes for us with groanings too deep for words" (Romans 8:26). The Holy Spirit takes the groanings of the soul and puts them into words. He helps us in our intercession.

Then find a friend who will believe you. Perhaps it will be someone who has also experienced abuse, though that is not necessary. There are many fine Christians who can sympathize though they themselves have never experienced the same trauma. You will need the strength of the Body of Christ in order to be healed.

At night,
unkissed, a-bed
without
anyone's blessing,
the weeping child
shudders and
sobs until
she's wrung dry
from tears,
and spent.

In the morning,
carefully,
she gathers the
tattered edges of
her garment
of composure
about her nakedness,
and tiptoes out
into another loveless day.

Oh, tell her about the One
Who promises
"I will never leave you
or forsake you,"
for
"I have loved you
with an
everlasting
love."

(Nancy Spiegelberg)

Dear Dorie:

I have never told anyone about my past that I shared with you and didn't realize how deeply it was hidden inside of me. As I was sharing bits of my past and actually said each one, the Lord pulled those aches out by the roots and healed them. In the days that followed I could sense a change within me.

Love,
L.

2
Confronting My Past

In November 1988 I invited my daughter, Darlene, and my grandson Derek to come with me to the orphanage in Oakland where my mother had left my sister and me, visiting us only twice in seven years. There I was beaten every night for misbehaving—sometimes justly but often for nothing at all. Worse, I was also sexually abused on numerous occasions. This is the story I've finally decided to tell.

The building has since been transformed into an art institute where students come to study and paint. With a mixture of apprehension and excitement we rang the doorbell.

A kind woman granted us permission to walk through the building, accompanying us because many of the doors were locked to insure the safety of the exhibits. I found myself describing to Darlene and the woman many of the changes that had taken place since the days when it had been an orphanage. Some of the original walls had been torn down to make larger rooms. Other walls had been remodeled, and the old green tile that I remembered so well was covered with new flooring. I walked through what had once been the dining room and opened the door that led to the parlor. Sitting in this room on a folding chair many years ago, I had opened my heart to God's love. I recalled the words of the student, "Remember, God loves you!"

We walked upstairs through two large swinging doors and into the room where we had slept. Darlene stood in front of the long window and called out, "Mom, is this where your bed stood?"

"Yes."

"Was that the door to Miss Gabriel's room?"

"Yes, honey."

"Mom, will you come over here?" When I crossed the room, she put her arms around me, and Derek joined us as we wept together. "I love you so much," she said.

We went into every room. We saw the long, narrow closet with partitions where our clothes had been hung; we went into the room where we used to dress. The original mirror with a crack in it was still on the wall, just as I had remembered. I had often sneaked into the dressing area to wet down my curly hair, trying to comb it in various ways to make myself more "adoptable." But no parents ever chose me to go home with them.

Off to the right were the two lavatories, one used by the matrons, the other used by us. Though one had been changed into an office, the woman let me open the door. "Darlene! There it is!" I shouted.

The original green floor that I remembered so vividly was still visible. Darlene stared down at the linoleum she had heard so much about. We stepped back, and I took a picture of it.

We continued down the hall. I pointed out the sewing room and the infirmary—the only place where we had been treated well. At the end of the hall was one more door, but I turned away, wanting to retrace my steps.

"Wouldn't you like to see this room?" the woman asked.

"Not particularly." No, I really didn't want to see that room. Darlene had heard me talk about life in the orphanage dozens of times, but there was one bit of information that I had kept from her. I wasn't sure whether I wanted to tell the rest of the story right now.

"Will you come, please?" the woman persisted.

I followed her, inwardly resisting. With her hand on the doorknob, she asked, "Can you tell us what happened here?"

Suddenly I found myself revealing the secret I had shared only with Lloyd. By now a number of art students had joined our tour, interested in the building's shrouded past. "This is the room where sexual abuse took place," I said.

She opened the door. The room had been remodeled. I explained that in the corner there used to be a toilet, and when I was naughty the matron would put my head in the bowl and flush it, warning me that my eyes and teeth would fall out when it was flushed. As the water swirled around my head and eyes, I would blow air, frantically trying to keep the water from coming up my nose.

Nearby was a closet with hooks on the wall. When I was there, rope was tied around my hands and then wrapped over the hooks. There I hung, supposedly as punishment for my misdeeds.

I spared the group the sordid details. The part-time matron responsible for these abuses used to take me into this room and force me to participate in sexual activities with her. She was tough, overweight, and spoke in a harsh voice. She would grab me by the neck and slam my head against the wall. When she twisted my arms and legs and threatened cruel punishment, I had no option but to do as she ordered. No one had to tell me that such unnatural sexual experiences were wrong. Thankfully, that matron was eventually dismissed from her responsibilities and institutionalized. But memories of those horrible experiences dogged me for years.

"Do you know why this room has been renovated?" the woman asked. "Because years ago it caught fire," she explained, answering her own question.

"The judgment of God!" I said impulsively. I didn't look at Darlene because I knew there were tears in her eyes. The woman smiled. As she closed the door, she commented, "I have to say something—I notice that there is no bitterness on your face and no hate in your voice."

"No, ma'am. You see, downstairs in the parlor, years ago, I met a Man named Jesus, and over a period of time He took away the bitterness and the hate. And now I am whole."

She closed the door, looked at the others who had joined us, and said, "Everything this woman has said has been verified by others who lived here. They have told the same story."

I now glanced at Darlene, who had tears running down her cheeks. "Darlene, your mother has been telling the truth all these years."

"I know, I know!" she replied.

"But it's good to know that others have authenticated it."

Until then, Darlene had not known that I had been sexually abused in the orphanage. But the woman's verification was further evidence that my life story was indeed true. To me it was as if God had put His stamp of approval on all that I had been telling others for many years. Now I could tell the whole story without fearing that people would not believe me.

Our tour of the orphanage had come to an end, so I waited until everyone had headed for the lobby. Then I returned alone to the door of that room, put my hand on it, and prayed. Tears flowed down my face as I spoke to my heavenly Father, my Friend who had saved me in that very building so many years ago. "Lord, thank You for letting me take this one last look at my past. Thank You for letting me know that all this is behind me. Thank You that I know that You have touched me and made me whole."

That day as the woman closed the door to that last room, she didn't realize how firmly she was closing the door to an ugly chapter of my life. It was as if the past were forever put behind me and I could say "It's all right." And it enabled me to allow God to use me to help others close the same door.

At a family retreat where I was speaking, a woman pulled me off to the side, opened her purse, and laid a picture on the table. My mouth fell open in disbelief. In the picture several girls were standing in a row. I recognized the Oakland orphanage in the background. "Do I know you?" I asked.

"Do you see the girl standing beside your friend? Well, that's me. I was in the same orphanage," she explained. We calculated the years we had each been there. She had left the orphanage about three years before I'd arrived. We had shared some of the same friends.

Here is her story.

She was born into a family of six children. Her mother fell ill and eventually became mentally disturbed, requiring that she be put into an insane asylum. Because none of the relatives could take all six children, they were divided up among the relatives and friends. This woman was given to a family that was sharing a home with another family.

Between the ages of six and nine she was repeatedly beaten and raped by the two men in the house. When her mother died, the children were redistributed, and the two families were informed that she would be taken away. The two men took her into a room to give her a final warning: "If you ever tell what we have done, this is what we are going to do—"

They took a razor blade and scraped her arm until it bled. Taking skin from either side of her neck, they nailed her to the floor with long, skinny nails. Then they pulled the nails out.

Her aunt came and took her to the orphanage in Oakland. For whatever reason, the head matron referred to this nine-year-old as "the dirty, little girl."

Because the children were required to leave the orphanage at the age of twelve, the same aunt returned three years later. She dropped the child off at the door of a girls' home and said, "I don't care where you go. You can either go in there or go out on the streets, but I don't ever want to see your face again."

She chose to enter the girls' home, doing the basic chores and learning to adjust as well as she could. Then she went into a foster home to work. But she was unloved by the families she served. Sometimes as she walked the streets, she paused at a neighborhood church, but she didn't go inside. She was a "dirty, little girl," and churches were for "good, clean people." No one ever invited her in.

She married as a teenager and had several children, but her marriage was a disaster. At the age of twenty-six she was noticed by a storekeeper in a little town in Texas. "You're new here. Why don't you come to church with us?" That day the pastor told the story of God's love. This woman says she picked up her child like a bag of sugar and went forward during the invitation to receive Christ as Savior.

"But," she said, "I didn't share my story with anyone. Nor did I study the Bible or grow in my faith. Finally somebody gave me a copy of your book, and I could hardly believe it. I realized that I had grown up in the same orphanage as you. I thought, *If only I could meet her!*"

Why had this woman kept her sordid story to herself for nearly forty years? She was afraid that no one would believe her, that no one would understand. She said she could share her story with me because she knew I would listen, and she knew I would believe her.

"Oh, honey," I said, "I have heard you not only with my ears but also with my heart!"

Like a broken dam, a torrent of tears coursed down her cheeks and fell upon her blouse. I held her in my arms.

"I hurt so much inside," she whispered when she had regained her composure.

"If I show you how, will you give the hurts to the Lord?"

"Yes, I will."

She poured it all out to God—the pain, the sexual abuse, the failed marriage, the loneliness, and the rejection.

I asked if I could share her story at the meeting the next evening. She agreed. She sat on the second chair from the aisle, keeping the next chair for me. After I had told her story to the audience, she shouted loudly enough for people to hear, "Dorie, I'm free!"

"Yes, those who are free in the Lord are free indeed!" I responded.

Why did she at long last experience such freedom? Because the secret was out. She no longer had to hide the guilt and hurt that she had privately carried all those years. Someone who knew all about her still loved and accepted her.

If it is true that we are only as sick as our darkest secrets, it is time that we begin to face the secrets that cast a pall of darkness on our lives. For those who are willing to admit their past, there is the possibility of healing and hope.

David said, "Search me, O God, and know my heart; try me and know my anxious thoughts; and see if there be any hurtful way in me, and lead me in the everlasting way" (Psalm 139:23-24). The first step is to ask the Holy Spirit to help us recall the hidden secrets of the past. It is much better to confront the enemy than to run away. Better to know what plagues us than to pretend that our past does not exist.

I do not believe, however, that we must relive our past hurts in minute detail. I've known individuals who have had years of therapy, carefully uncovering sordid details that go back to infancy. Yet many of these people have been unable to cope with the gamut of feelings that have surfaced as a result. We must acknowledge that the past has happened, but we also need to know what to do when the hurt comes to the surface.

Talk to your heavenly Father first. He is well acquainted with your past. He can fill in the details that you might overlook. Even if words fail you, the Holy Spirit will give you the help you need.

Then find a friend who can help you. In this book we will meet several people who kept their pasts hidden and therefore suffered emotional consequences. We must begin by talking to God, but we also need the acceptance and love of other people.

Though I had long since shut the door on my past, the day I visited the orphanage in Oakland I closed it one last time—forever. Thankfully, I am no longer held hostage to what happened there. And my new friend is on her way to freedom, too.

Dear Dorie:

I'm 28 years old. . . . My mother tried to kill me as a baby. . . . My scars are very deep. I have been a basket case on drugs, living like the dead. Though I met Jesus and fell in love with Him, I was still very insane, so hurt and shattered. There was no instant healing, but gradually God has healed me. One of the biggest healings came when I heard you speak—this is why I say I love you. You have given me hope. . . . God is using you to shine a ray of bright hope to a scared, sad, and sorrowing heart.

Love,
S.

3

The Power of Hope

As a young woman, I frequently wondered what effect the abuse I had experienced would have on the rest of my life. Would others find out about my secret? Would I be able to enjoy sex if I ever married?

In those days sexual abuse was not talked about as openly as it is today. Even as I approached my twenties and entered Bible college, I lived with a swirl of painful thoughts. Not even my close friends knew what I had experienced. I seldom talked about the physical abuse, much less the sexual abuse. The memories were too painful. What is more, I didn't think anyone would believe me.

What helped me though those difficult years of self-doubt was the confidence that God would be with me through it all. I had something that many others do not have—*hope*.

Abused children often are convinced that they are ruined for the rest of their lives. They will actually put themselves in situations where they must play the role of a victim; it is a role they think they deserve. They become locked into a vicious cycle and think that there is no hope of escape.

A woman abused by an alcoholic father often ends up marrying a man who is like her father. Unconsciously—perhaps even consciously—she is saying, "I deserved abuse as a child, and I continue to deserve it as an adult." There is an actual *bonding* to the abuse, which causes her to actively play the role of a victim. She has no plans to rise above her situation and is devoid of all hope for a better life.

In extreme cases, a passive victim actually looks for someone to abuse her. She becomes so convinced that she deserves ill treatment that she rejects genuine love when it is offered her. Usually she makes life so difficult for the one who wants to love her that further rejection becomes inevitable.

Others play an aggressive role in the inflicting of torment. They look for people whom they can harm, convincing themselves that their victims deserve it. Sometimes rapists try to pin the blame for their crimes on the women, claiming it their fault because they were out walking alone.

Abusers cannot consciously bear the thought that they are responsible for the awful act of sexually abusing a child. They either deny that they did it, or they find some reason to claim that the child was really responsible. In either case they find some rationalization to justify their actions.

When bonding to abusive behavior occurs, victims of sexual or physical abuse inflict the same punishment upon their own children. Either actively or passively, abuse victims often may perpetuate the abuse.

One of my desires is to help people break out of what Andre Bustanoby calls "the ruined woman syndrome." This term refers to those who accept the role of a ruined woman and play out whatever they believe to be the logical consequences of their trauma. Some women become prostitutes, convinced that they are already morally stained and therefore have no reason to live chaste lives. They are convinced that their condition cannot be improved and that they are condemned to live the life of ruined women. If they do not go into prostitution, they live out the same attitude in other destructive ways. Unfortunately, such victims often avoid any attempt to begin the long, painful process of recovery. In one way or another they have taught themselves to be content as victims—instead of as survivors.

The Way to Hope

I have found that it is not enough simply to tell the hurting that there is hope. Usually they are filled with such cynicism that words alone ring hollow. Often they have already adopted one of the usual coping methods: denial or disassociation.

Denial is a psychological mechanism that enables some victims to deny that they were abused. Reality is too painful—the fact that someone they trusted could betray them is too difficult to handle. So the child tells himself or herself that it is all a dream, that it is not happening. Denial can continue years after the fact.

Disassociation is separating the memory from conscious recall. A victim may not remember what happened because the pain has been buried deep in the subconscious. The memories are buried. In matters of abuse, the person develops complete amnesia.

These defenses are best overcome when the victim hears someone else tell a story of abuse. That often triggers memories that have been deeply buried, and the person who has lived with denial or disassociation is forced to face reality. That is why I share my own story. Some people have told me that they were unable to read my previous book, *Dorie*, because it revived memories that were too painful. Others have walked out of meetings in which I was telling my life story. Confronting the past is difficult but necessary in the healing process. Hearing the experiences of a victim who has become a survivor gives hope to those who struggle. When they see that others have experienced abuse and have recovered—when they see someone with a similar background finding emotional and spiritual wholeness—many receive their first glimmer of hope. The door of the prison opens just a little.

We must also remind victims that any guilt they feel is *false guilt*. The girl who feels guilty because of what her father did to her is innocent. Likewise the boy who feels intense shame for the abuse from his neighbor—he did not deserve what happened.

Studies have shown that those who were aggressors or willing victims in the relationship have a more difficult time putting their past behind them. They may not view their guilt as false since they were to some degree accomplices in the sexual relationship. However, it is obvious that an abuser may sometimes arouse the sexual feeling of his victim. That is understandable since we are sexual beings. Regardless, the victim is not responsible for or guilty of the actions of the abuser.

I've counseled many who think that they are too sinful for God to forgive them. They feel condemned, contaminated by the weight of their own sinfulness. To every one of them we must offer the grace of God in Christ. *There is no sin you or anyone else has committed that is too great for God to forgive*. Christ came to sinners—not to those who think they are righteous. To say that anyone is too sinful is to minimize the value of Christ's death on the cross—a death that God received as a payment for all sin. Hope is available to everyone.

We must create a climate of acceptance, an atmosphere that is open and understanding. Those of us who have experienced abuse can lead the way by becoming vulnerable ourselves and by being honest about how we feel about our pasts and the struggles we still have. And we must be willing to listen as the hurt and anger of the past spill out. We need to affirm that anyone can give up her or his self-image as a ruined person. But that can only happen as people become willing to talk and to honestly face their past.

A slave who has been beaten and deprived finds it difficult to look up into the sky. He is bound to the earth, preoccupied with his menial duties and hardships. His eyes are focused downward, not upward. Yet whether he looks at it or not, the sky is there, just as God is with us whether we acknowledge Him or not. We must help those who have been abused to look away from themselves for at least a few brief moments. They must learn to see themselves differently; they must substitute their current self-portrait with the one found in the New Testament.

Anyone who trusts Christ as Savior receives God's special grace, which is "freely bestowed on us in the Beloved" (Ephesians 1:6). Believers are elevated to "heirs of God and fellow heirs with Christ" (Romans 8:17). I can't tell you how often these and other verses have come to mind as I have thought about my own painful past. In my younger years they were all I had to go on; they enabled me to believe that God accepted me, even though my parents didn't.

It is not easy to accept all that we are in Christ. Those of us with scarred backgrounds balk at the idea of being called perfect in Christ. We struggle with the fact that the Almighty gives special attention to His children. We even become convinced that those lofty advantages cannot really be ours.

But they are! We must learn to believe God's promises for us rather than our negative feelings and clouded emotions. That's when the transformation process begins. As we learn to understand God's generosity toward us, we will spend more time in praise to God. Only through the Holy Spirit and the Word of God can we have insight into the privileged relationship possible with Jesus Christ.

Ethel Waters, who died at age eighty, became well known through her singing at numerous Billy Graham crusades. She was the product of a rape relationship—a fourteen-year-old girl was raped, and Ethel was conceived.

About her background she said, "A child growing up needs a lap to cuddle up in. That never happened to me. Never. It's a . . . tragic hurt, wanting to be wanted so bad."

Yet after she became a Christian she said, "I keep praising the Lord so much that I don't have any other hobbies!" One of her favorite songs was "His Eye Is on the Sparrow." His eye is truly on every sparrow.

Following are the stories of two young women who were caught up in the awful cycle of playing the part of a victim; however, they were rescued by the power of Christ. There is hope. Our identity *can* be changed. We *can* see ourselves as loved and beautiful. Bit by bit the past loses its power over us as we look away from ourselves to Christ.

Two Examples

The first woman wrote me a letter about her painful past: "My father was forced to marry my mother because of an unwanted child (me). I grew up with hatred. I was sexually abused by my mother's men friends. My father told me how ugly I was; and he would beat me."

A few paragraphs later the letter continues, "I met a boy who is now my husband and became pregnant. We married and had trouble from day one. He beat me. I was rebellious and felt unloved by him."

Then comes a short but powerful sentence, "After four years of torture, God saved us." She goes on to say that with the help of her pastor and a Christian psychologist, she now has a stable marriage. In fact, her mother and father have both become Christians. "The hate is gone," she writes. "Now I too have the joy, peace, and happiness of God's unending love." Not bad for an illegitimate child who was both sexually and physically abused!

The second example is a woman who writes, "I was sexually abused by all three of my brothers and several other people in the family. I sought . . . my love through drugs, sex, and alcohol. In 1976 while pregnant out of wedlock, I cried out to God, and He heard." Fortunately that is not the end of the story. "Now I am married and have three children. . . . My husband and I have been living for the Lord for seven years. [I] give my testimony on how God delivered me from the effects of sexual abuse and drugs. I praise the Lord for taking the foolish things and making something out of them."

Of course the change in the lives of these women was difficult, and it took time. But it happened because we have a great God.

Many of us can say that though we were once victims, we are now survivors. Stuart Hamblin used to sing the song "It Is No Secret [What God Can Do]." What God has done for me, He can do for anyone. There is life beyond abuse. "Therefore if any man is in Christ, he is a new creature; the old things passed away; behold, new things have come" (2 Corinthians 5:17).

The first step toward recovery is to begin to hope.

Jesus,
They say
ugly people hit You
and spit on You
and called You names.
They made fun of You
and laughed and teased
and took away Your clothes.

They say
You cried—real loud—
and wondered why
Your Pappa left You
alone
when You were hurting
so bad
that You could die.

Did anyone ever call You
an abused child?
That's what they say I am.

I guess You understand.
(Nancy Spiegelberg)

Dear Dorie:

Dorie, how I wish you were here by my side so that I could pour out my heart to you. Others don't understand my pain because they have never been there.

Love,
S.

Dear Dorie:

Dorie, please don't think that girls are the only ones who are abused. There are plenty of boys who are Dories too—and I'm one of them.

Love,
T.

4
The Power of a Listening Ear

One evening in Portland I returned to my hotel room, tired after a day of ministry. As I walked into the room I noticed an unsigned note that had been pushed under the door. "I wanted to isolate you all to myself—to grab you and not let anyone else near you . . . you knew me; you spoke my words. Many of your lonely moments were *mine*," the note began.

"'They' could not possibly understand. 'They've' always been loved, accepted, and understood. 'They've' always had someone they belonged to, but you and I never did.

"But once we knew Him, we knew that He loved us and no one could ever take Him away! They could *never, never* touch our souls again. He had us for eternity. . . . We dance to a different tune, a different drum. His drum!

"But sometimes we know the meaning of the groanings and moanings of our soul—the times when voices and words do not exist. Yet He is our voice to God, our interpreter . . . our soothing salve—our 'tiger balm.' Praise God for you!"

What that lady expressed is all too true—there are some people who can better understand the hurts of others because they themselves have been hurt. As for others, "they" may never understand.

After hundreds of meetings throughout the United States and abroad, I am convinced that this hurting world needs a listening ear. "Dorie... I wish you were right here by my side so that I could pour out my heart to you" expresses the feelings of many others. People are looking for someone who will believe them, someone who can say, "I've been through it, too. I know how you feel."

The art of listening is difficult to learn in our society. We are often in such a hurry that we don't have time to listen to other people's problems. Impatience is the foe of a listening heart.

A second barrier that must be overcome is the feeling that we have *the* answer to a person's problem and that he or she simply needs to understand some biblical truth. We are tempted to think we have all the answers. Clearly, truth is important, but from personal experience I know that sometimes I just need someone to feel my hurt and share my pain. It's not enough to *speak;* a friend must also *feel.* A good listener can take the weight of another's burden upon himself without saying much more than a single word. When you leave the presence of such a friend, your burden feels lighter. A friend like that can truly share your sorrows.

Let me share some of my mail with you, some letters that tell of hurt and healing. I don't want you to focus on the pain (though it is important to understand the hurts of others), but rather on the principles that can make the emotionally wounded whole. In each instance notice that the healing process began when the individual found a friend she could talk to—someone who listened and cared.

As you read the first letter, look beyond the words to the hurt that she felt for most of her life. Remember the hope that Christ offers, which can be the means of bringing sunshine into a dark life.

My father abandoned me, and later my mother was remarried to a bigger drunk than my father. I listened to my mother get beat up so many times I cannot shut out her cries, even today. I was molested and had no one to reach out to me in kindness.

I hated myself, my name, and the very breath I took. By age 5, I didn't want to live anymore.

I accepted Christ at age 17; by then I was already married and the mother of a child. Why did I accept Him? Because He said He would set me free! "I have come that you might have life and have it more abundantly," He said.

The joy never came. I am 45 now, and I find it hard to trust anyone, not even God. I don't want to be hurt anymore. My husband committed suicide; that hurt so bad, I didn't want to put my children through that a second time.

But . . . God is all I have and when I put my trust in Him, I know I must leave it in His hands. I'm seeing a counselor, a lovely man in the Lord. Dorie, he really listens; it feels so good to have someone who cares. I always had taken the blame for everything that happened in my life. Now I am finding out that I wasn't responsible—my parents and others were. I have to forgive them, but the pain and hurts are raw.

Dorie, I cry out to God to help me find the peace I've searched for since I received Him. I think the key is forgiveness, but it is going to take time.

I've hidden the truth from myself for so long; I have to get used to the idea that it wasn't my fault. But how do I keep the memories from hurting so much?

Love
L.

Whether she realizes it or not, this woman is on the way to recovery. She has made some important breakthroughs. Despite her past disappointments with Christ, she may yet find that He is as good as His Word.

Let's look back over that letter. In it are some reasons to hope that eventually this woman's past will no longer control her future.

She realizes that she is not responsible for what happened to her. Virtually every abused child assumes he or she is at fault for the abuse endured. The reason for that misplaced guilt is not hard to fathom. It is difficult to admit that one's parents were criminals. God has placed within every child a profound respect for his mother and father. This bond of affection is so strong that there is almost nothing parents can do to shatter it. The idea that the father and mother, who gave physical life, could abandon and abuse their child is difficult to accept. Thus, when a little child is abused, he comes to the conclusion that his parents are doing what is right and that he is simply getting what he deserves. *My parents are responding to me as they ought to*, he thinks. *Any parent would do the same thing with a child as awful as I am.* In this way the child himself assumes the responsibility and the accompanying guilt. The burden becomes unbearable.

The result? The child feels so dirty and so ashamed that he or she wants to die. That is why the average age of suicide victims is decreasing in our society. Children are killing themselves.

No child should *ever* bear the responsibility for the sins of his or her parents. A friend used to say that God will never hold us responsible for having done a poor job of raising our parents!

Second, the woman who wrote that letter understands that she must forgive her parents. Difficult though that will be, it is absolutely necessary for her emotional recovery.

The process of forgiveness can be expedited if she understands that her anger toward her parents must be mixed with pity. Many parents are bound by emotional deficiencies that drive them to abuse their children. As I pointed out in the last chapter, those who were abused as children often repeat the same behavior.

It is almost impossible for a child abuser even to admit his need for help. Indeed, without God's intervention, there is little hope for a reversal of his cruel behavior patterns. Imagine what it must be like to have perverted drives and to be obsessed by those desires to the point that they are beyond your control. Once these lusts are acted out, it is easier to repeat the behavior a second time—and a third and a fourth. Meanwhile, the heart becomes hardened, calloused, and indifferent. All human kindness is gone. One must pity such depravity.

There is also a third ray of hope in this woman's quest for peace. She has found a listening ear, someone who is willing to bear her hurt, to understand, and to care. Evidently her counselor has not had an abusive background, but he is taking time to understand, sympathize, and aid her in learning how to bear her burdens.

Imagine what it would be like to be trapped in your own emotional prison without anyone to talk to, without anyone willing to take the time and effort to understand you. More than anything you'd want a friend to stand with you and cry with you. If you were carrying a one-hundred-pound bag of potatoes, you would find it wonderful to meet a fellow-traveler who agreed to carry part of the load. Two people could carry that sack more easily than one. You may be saying, "But I'm the one who endured the injustice." Granted, part of the burden can only by carried by the one who endured the abuse. But I know from experience that sharing our needs with someone who cares lightens any load. Christ said that His yoke was easy, His burden light. When we discover that we are not alone in the struggle and find others who have faced the same abuse, we can take heart. To know that you are a part of a large family of hurting people brings a ray of hope.

But why has not this woman experienced the peace Christ offers? Why does God heal some people more dramatically than others? His grace is adequate for everyone, but what may be needed is the decision to forgive and the total surrender of her life to God.

Read the following letter, and you will understand what I mean. Though this woman experienced many of the same abuses as the one above, she has come further in the healing process.

> I had the same abuse as you did as a child. Only my mother tried to kill me four times. Twice she tried drowning me, and the other two times were in the car. My father tried to molest me. At 15 I was taken from my parents. . . . I came to know Christ as my Savior at 16.
>
> Next was my marriage. I found out that my husband was a homosexual and after a while my marriage ended in divorce. Later I remarried and had to go to the hospital because my husband beat me. The physical abuse got so bad that I wound up in a nursing home with a nervous breakdown.
>
> From then on, it was drinking, smoking, and drugs . . . I attempted suicide seven or eight times . . . I have seen so many psychiatrists . . . doctors told me that I wouldn't live long because my body is falling apart and my nerves are so bad. I was looking forward to death.
>
> I read your book and cried because it brought all the pain to the surface . . . all I could think about was why I couldn't have the kind of peace you have . . . but I was afraid.
>
> I finally called a friend from my church who came over. I made a total commitment of life to the Lord. That night all—and I mean all—the pain disappeared . . . all my confusion vanished. I [had] never felt so good.
>
> Since then I have been leaving all my problems at the cross. I have peace with God and full assurance about my salvation. Never in my wildest dreams did I ever think I could be so happy.

If I had never read your book I never would have returned to my precious Lord. I praise the Lord for guiding you in the writing of it.

Love
J.

That is proof that there can be life beyond abuse!

Recognizing Where Healing Begins

Perhaps you have no one to talk to. Perhaps you have a friend who listens but does not understand the depth of your hurt. Let me encourage you to begin with God. Christ is the wonderful Counselor who can be trusted with confidential information. He can say, "Yes, I know about your situation. I understand completely." In hundreds of places the Bible says that the Lord *heard* the prayers of His people. He is listening!

"I waited patiently for the Lord; and He inclined to me, and heard my cry," wrote David (Psalm 40:1). When the ground moved under him, the Lord was listening. Regarding the children of Israel, we read that the Lord "heard their groanings" (Exodus 2:24). He did not turn a deaf ear to their cries when they were beaten as slaves. God has a listening ear!

Dear Dorie:

In August of this year I spent 4 days in a mental hospital. All my life I was neglected, rejected, and abused, and so was on medication for nerves by the time I reached 17. I have lived with nightmares, fears, restlessness, hate, and was unable to enjoy a normal life of happiness. I became spiteful and hated those who rejected me and abused me. Twice I wanted to kill myself, but the Lord kept me in His hand. . . . Now I am happy. It was your ministry to the ladies that made me pray, "Lord, You've done it for Dorie, now do it for me." And He did. I have never felt so free, and people that know me tell me they see the change—I smile a lot, and I'm able to love others. I'm not afraid because I feel the Holy Spirit is with me. Now I'm trying to help my son deal with the hurts in his life, for I was not the mother I should have been for him. If I could only shout to everyone about my freedom, I would. Often I have the urge to run and hug people I meet on the street and tell them what God did for me and that He can do the same for them.

Love,
S.

5
The Power of a Loving Touch

When I was growing up, I was not allowed to sit on my mother's lap. When my younger sister, who was much prettier than I, came to my mother, she would be picked up; I was pushed away like an unwanted dog. At that early age I knew the pain of rejection—the pain of having no one to give you a loving touch. I grew to understand the power of touch. I craved the love that could be communicated through a tender hug or a touch on the arm. An appropriate, loving touch says, "I love you, and I care."

Gary Smalley describes the long-lasting influence of a single loving caress in the life of Marilyn Monroe. She was conceived out of wedlock, and in her early years she was shuffled from one foster home to another. One day after she had become famous as a sex goddess, a reporter asked if she'd ever felt loved by the foster families with whom she lived. "Once," she replied, "when I was about seven or eight. The woman I was living with was putting on makeup, and I was watching her. She was in a happy mood, so she reached over and patted my cheeks with her rouge puff. . . . For that moment, I felt loved by her." Though the touch lasted but a few seconds, the memory of it still brought tears to Marilyn Monroe's eyes. As Gary Smalley says, "As small an act as it was, it was like pouring buckets of love and security on the parched life of a little girl starved for affection" (*The Blessing* [Nashville: Thomas Nelson, 1986], pp. 43-44; Smalley quoted Monroe's story from Helen Colton, *The Gift of Touch* [New York: Seaview/Putnam, 1983] p. 49).

Only God knows the number of young women who have fallen into sexual promiscuity because they were starved for affection. Many a girl has testified that immorality was simply the price she had to pay to be held and, in the words of one, "to mean something to someone."

Researchers have gone so far as to suggest that if we could better analyze and understand the kind of physical contact a child receives, we could predict the future emotional health of the child. Of course we must always make room for the grace of God. Our heavenly Father can reverse the deprivations of our childhood. But the power of a loving touch cannot be overstated.

Along with the emotional and spiritual benefits of human touch, there are physical benefits as well. A touch can increase the hemoglobin of the body. Touch allows the tissues to receive more oxygen and lowers one's blood pressure. A UCLA study estimated that if married couples were to give each other between eight and ten meaningful touches per day, they might live up to two years longer.

Because we are sexual creatures, I am often asked about the dangers of physical touch between men and women or between a father and his daughter. I am well aware that there is such a thing as a sensual touch that could become negative or dangerous. My answer to such fears is that we should not allow Satan to rob us of one of God's gifts to His people just because it can be abused. To give a hug as an expression of Christian love can often be therapy to an aching heart.

The Example of Christ

A story in the gospel of Mark illustrates Christ's willingness to touch the untouchable. It is difficult for us to imagine the loathsomeness of leprosy. The victim experienced lethargy and pain. Discolored patches appeared over his body. Pink and brown nodules appeared and ulcerated, emitting a foul discharge. The voice became hoarse, the breath wheezing. The head became contorted, causing the person to appear almost inhuman. Finally, nerve fibers became infected, causing a loss of sensation. Eventually fingers and toes fell off. In short the leper became a hideous sight. According to the Old Testament regulations, he was to tear his clothes and cry, "Unclean! Unclean!" whenever others came near. He did not even have the right to speak to other human beings. Eventually, he would die in loneliness.

With a cry of desperation, the leper in Mark 1 says, "If You are willing, You can make me clean" (v. 40). His plea was not just for healing but also for significance. He wanted to matter to somebody.

Christ had compassion on him. He did the unthinkable—the Son of God reached out to touch the leper. Christ could have healed the man without touching him, but the Savior wanted to identify Himself with this poor, hapless soul. Along with the touch, Christ spoke these words, "I am willing; be cleansed" (v. 41). The leper probably never forgot those gracious words. If you are emotionally starved, you will not forget words of love and encouragement spoken to you by friends or relatives.

THE UNTOUCHABLES TODAY

Who are the untouchables of today? They may not appear to be untouchable; in fact, they may look very attractive. But many people do *feel* untouchable; inside they are starving for acceptance and love.

The first group are those of us who have been physically and sexually abused. Let me remind you that individuals who fit this description sometimes need time before they can accept the loving touch of another human being. If you have befriended such a survivor, don't assume that he or she automatically wants to be touched. Often they will even cringe at the thought of an innocent hug or touch on the arm.

Don't force the issue. Remember that for many of us touch was often a painful experience. We were betrayed by the very people who should have protected us. We were whipped, not wanted. If you have a continuing friendship with a survivor, let her tell you when she is ready to be hugged. Be sensitive to her feelings in the matter. Progress is often slow, but it is sure.

Following is a letter from a woman who is confined within her emotional and spiritual prison; yet a loving touch gave her a ray of hope:

> I am a vegetable. I can't even do the housework, or so I tell myself. I sit all day and read, drink, and smoke. I live in a pig sty and smell like it. Most of the time I seem to be oblivious to the filth until someone comes to the door or our ceiling caves in (as it has just done). My drinking does not seem to bother me until I have chest pains. I have a bad heart.
>
> I have even tried reading 3 psalms a day as you suggested.
>
> The other night I was at the meeting where you spoke. I couldn't talk to you in front of all those people. I just couldn't. My ex-pastor's wife was there, and if I ever broke down in front of her, I would never go out in public again.
>
> I was hugged and told I was loved recently by a cousin who was visiting. Well, it turned something loose in me. I want to write to her and tell her I love her too, but I'm scared. She might not want to see me again. I was terribly embarrassed, but I got over it.
>
> Love
> C.

Yes, a loving hug can turn something loose inside those who have been abused. It can give us a sense of security and can make us feel wanted and acceptable. The abused need a loving touch.

Second, divorced people also need the compassion of a loving touch. As I talk to divorcees, I find that one partner often feels rejected and unclean. I have discovered that there are often innocent victims—a woman whose husband leaves for another woman or a man whose wife decides she needs to be free from marriage to "find herself." Those who are left behind usually feel intense rejection. Divorce is a tremendous blow to one's personhood. One woman said that when she came to church the Sunday after the divorce was final, she felt as if a capital D had been branded on her forehead. Divorced! Unclean! Victims of divorce must be reminded that they are valued members of the Body of Christ. Often a simple touch is all it takes to communicate that message.

A third group of untouchables is AIDS victims. Granted, many victims have contracted this deadly disease through homosexuality or unclean needles used for drugs. Even so, these twentieth-century lepers desperately need the love and the compassion of Christ.

After one of my seminars, a handsome young man stayed to talk with me. He had his head in his hands. He said to me, "Dorie, my mother threw me out into the street when I was nine years old; she didn't want me. I wandered about trying to earn a living and became involved in homosexuality. A year ago I became a Christian. I left my former lifestyle. I went in for testing, and I found out I have AIDS. I'm going to die. I'm so scared. Dorie, please tell me . . . please tell me that I am forgiven! Tell me that I have been forgiven!"

I showed him Isaiah 44:22 where we are assured that our sins have been blotted out: "I have wiped out your transgressions like a thick cloud, and your sins like a heavy mist. Return to Me, for I have redeemed you." Then I took him into my arms and held him as if he were my own son. As his tears fell onto my sweater, he said, "Dorie! Nobody touches me . . . my friends think they can get AIDS through my tears!"

Why did I hold him? Because that's what Christ would have done. He is no longer on earth physically to touch lepers. We now do it in His stead. "As the Father hath sent me, so send I you."

The Touch of God

In my early years I was considered the "ugly duckling"—the one who was "not adoptable." I watched many couples come to the orphanage to inspect all the children before they chose one to cherish as their very own. I could not blame them for not choosing me. Yet I had to wonder why God did not make me as pretty as Brenda or Patty—or Ruth.

As I grew in my understanding of Christ, I realized that I had to accept my features as gifts from God. Eventually I came to the point where I was able to thank God for my appearance.

A man reared in an alcoholic home said that he was never touched, held, or loved. His favorite passage of Scripture is Psalm 139:10: "Even there Thy hand will lead me, and Thy right hand will lay hold of me." He is encouraged to know that he was at least touched by the hand of God. That psalm also teaches that God fashioned each of us in our mother's womb. The same divine attention that was accorded Adam and Eve was also given to us; we were sculpted by God. He determined our features, and He formed us according to His desires and will.

All of us, however, want to be touched by a human being. We find it difficult to "settle for" the imperceptible touch of God. Yet, even as a teenager I discovered that God's presence can give us grace to bear the deep hurts of life. In the final analysis what really matters is whether or not we have been touched by the Almighty. "Though my father and my mother have forsaken me, the Lord will take me up."

How can we receive that divine touch? First, we must accept Christ as our own Savior; that is, we must come to God through His Son. That's the decision I made at the age of thirteen in the orphanage in Oakland. I told God that no human being wanted me, and if He wanted me He could have me! That was the first time I was ever touched by God.

Second, we experience the divine touch every day as we reassure ourselves of our acceptance through the promises of God and our own submission to His will. Hebrews 13:5-6 says, "I will never desert you, nor will I ever forsake you," so that we confidently say, "The Lord is my helper, I will not be afraid. What shall man do to me?"

Thankfully, we can know God's presence and His touch.

The Human Touch as Used by God

One day I was in the South where I met a woman who had a background of abuse. What I did not realize is that she was also unsure of her relationship with God, uncertain about whether or not He would ever accept her. I realized later that the hug I gave her allowed her to think it possible to be loved on earth and in heaven. My touch had introduced her to the touch of God:

> I grew up in a tar paper shack in a small town. My so-called mother was a real gem! She would beat and molest me—I think you call it incest now. She would use my Dad's razor strap or a broom handle. When you told about your being beaten with a belt, I cringed and felt every blow.
>
> When I did try to tell someone she would put me down into a trap door in the chicken coop. I was left in this hole, sometimes all night (even today I won't go into a dark room).

> When you told me you loved me and hugged me, it made me feel good. I never had a lady or a mother who ever did that. I am beginning to believe that it doesn't hurt to be hugged or touched if it's Christian people. I don't know much about that kind of life, but I do know that you ladies at the retreat are different.
>
> Dorie, in my 39 years I never had anyone like you say "I love you" and hug me. . . . I hope you really meant it. I feel like a little kid hoping that someone does care but yet I wonder what the motive is.
>
> Dorie, please write and tell us all about your Jesus. . . . I still can't get over how much love I felt there, even though I didn't know the songs they sang, but everything was so beautiful.
>
> You know, Dorie, if I ever get good enough for your God (and someday I will because my husband says we are going to try to find a church and buy a Bible and read it together) . . . if I get good enough to go to heaven, you know what I am going to do? I'm going to sit on Jesus' lap (I've never sat on anyone's lap) and ask Him to just hug me until it doesn't hurt anymore.

I think that is what many of us are going to do! Just sit on Jesus' lap and let Him hug us until it doesn't hurt anymore.

I wrote a letter to this woman explaining that my Jesus is even better than she thought. We do not have to be good enough to enter into heaven. All we have to do is accept Him as our own Savior, and He will qualify us to become God's children forever. "But as many as received Him, to them He gave the right to become children of God, even to those who believe in His name" (John 1:12).

Let's give this hurting world a loving touch. We do it on behalf of Christ, who came to heal our wounds and to put us back together. Our touch can be His touch to those who need to know the meaning of love.

By Extension

God,
I heard
Your arms have
extensions . . .
Or is it . . .
You have
extended arms?

God,
if You really
do have extended arms
down here—

Who are you
going to send
with Your
special-stretched-out
arms
to hug me today?
(Nancy Spiegelberg)

Dear Dorie:

Six weeks before I first heard you speak, I tried to take my life. I had experienced so many rejections, and the last one was just too much—my husband of 16 years left me. I spent eight weeks in the hospital, and they helped me to accept the rejection, but you helped me forgive. Two days before you came I was able to call my mother who had given me up for adoption at the age of 10. I told her I forgave her. Thank you for your testimony of forgiveness.

Love,
R.

6
The Power of Forgiveness

People who have been abused have numerous barriers to overcome in order to experience emotional and spiritual wholeness. Perhaps the most difficult barrier is the bitterness, hostility, and anger. Read my mail and you will begin to understand why so many people struggle with bitter, unforgiving spirits.

A twenty-nine-year-old woman wrote to me saying that she had been born prematurely at six months because her mother's attempts at abortion failed. She was hidden in the house until she was four years old because her mother was ashamed of her ugliness. She was pushed around and beaten until she started school. She never knew that some mothers didn't beat their children. She was not allowed to play with other children. Equally devastating, her mother never hugged her, never told her that she was loved, never wiped her tears away. Instead, that little girl was constantly ridiculed.

Her father moved out of the house but returned each day to chase his wife and demand that she give him "what she owed him," namely, sex.

One afternoon when she was nine years old, her father and three older brothers came home drunk. The father roared through the house looking for his wife, and when he could not find her he noticed his daughter on the bed. He told his sons that since he could not find "the old lady," he would get what he wanted from his little girl—all four of them agreed she was "ready."

That little girl ran and fought with all of her nine-year-old strength but was trapped by the men and carried to the bed. Her father and brothers argued over who should be first; the father insisted that it was his right since he had had the idea. With one brother holding her down, she was forced to perform oral sex; then she was raped by all four of them.

They warned her that she would be killed if she told anyone. Her oldest brother made her sit in a tub of water so that her mother would not suspect anything. Screaming in agony, she sat in the water. When her mother returned, she beat her daughter for not having cleaned the house.

Her mother falsely accused her of having an affair with an old man when she was eleven. Her mother told the principal at school about it, so the daughter was required to stay after hours. The punishment for this alleged crime was that the girl had to stand in the corner at military attention and stare at a 100-watt bulb without blinking. For the slightest twitch she was beaten.

When she was finally allowed to go to bed at 2:30 or 3:00 A.M., her feet were tied to the bed post. Her mother would awaken her, torturing her sexually to "see if you have been with Mr. X."

In her letter to me, this young lady says, "What amazes me is that the neighbors never asked any questions—and always thought of my mother as a sweet God-fearing old lady. I never told anyone about this until this letter, thinking they wouldn't believe me anyhow . . . who knows, maybe you won't either."

As a result of all her hurts the young woman flunked out of college (she could do the work but couldn't gather the emotional strength to attend classes) and turned to food to compensate for her lack of friends. Understandably, she is bitter. She says that if she had the courage she would kill her family. "I hate them," she says, "with a hatred that almost scares me."

The questions such a story raises are many and painful. How can this woman release the years of bitterness that have built up within her mind and soul? Can she do that, knowing that her family may never be called to account here on earth for what they have done? Is forgiveness realistic when the family has not even asked for it? How can this woman be freed from the emotional damage of such brutality?

This chapter is about a difficult concept—forgiveness. You may wonder how it can be possible to actually pardon the inflictors of the extreme cruelty you have experienced. A general understanding of how abusers become hardened to the point that they intentionally hurt little children may help resolve the anger you feel. Then forgiveness may begin.

The path toward moral debauchery usually begins with a series of small and seemingly insignificant decisions. But one step leads to another until all manner of perversions enter a man's life. Ted Bundy, a man who was executed for killing approximately twenty young women, candidly explained that he had become addicted to pornography. Eventually that habit did not satisfy him, so he turned to violence, which gave him the same euphoria as pornography. Only bizarre behavior could give him the sensational orgasm he craved. Bundy did not start out intending to be a pedophile or a murderer. He began with a sin he thought he could control but discovered that he could not master it. Instead, it mastered him.

Man contends with his fallen sinful nature; Bundy is evidence of that. But one's environment, particularly his home, also greatly influences his choices in life. If he grew up with abusive parents, he has a greater potential to abuse his children, just as he himself was abused. Why? Whether he realizes it or not, he is acting out his own hostility. He demeans his children just as he was demeaned; he sees himself in them and uses violence to express his own anger.

In addition, the Bible tells us that Satan is at work in the world. With his myriads of demons he controls the actions of evil men to some degree. He takes advantage of every opportunity to blind people to their real needs and directs them instead toward deceptive lusts.

Now put those three factors together: man's sinful nature, rejection from hostile or abusive parents, and the activity of Satan. That combination can lead a man into virtually any form of cruelty imaginable. Those factors allow a father to rape his defenseless nine-year-old daughter or a mother to attempt to drown her own flesh and blood. Reprehensible as these acts are, the fact is that many people are caught in the prison of their own desires and lusts.

In spite of the depths of evil within man, forgiveness is still essential to those who wish to overcome the devastation of their past. Some claim that we cannot forgive others until they ask for it; after all, we are told, the very concept of forgiveness requires that the offender seek reconciliation. But if that were true, most of us would still be holding onto our bitterness. Abusers seldom, if ever, ask for forgiveness. We must be willing to release the bitterness we hold against those who have wronged us, whether they ask for it or not. Forgiveness is necessary for our own well-being; it is not something we do solely for the benefit of the offender. Sometimes we must even forgive those who have died if we wish to experience inner healing.

I do want to make clear that each person must forgive at his or her own speed. Temperaments and circumstances vary so vastly that there can be no single formula that works for every person. Some can forgive their abusers rather quickly; for others it takes months and even years. But I do believe that every person can forgive and relinquish the bitterness —even the young woman described at the beginning of this chapter. If forgiveness seems to be impossible, let us remember that God helps us to do the impossible. Thankfully, God understands the nature of forgiveness, for He Himself has had to forgive many times.

Forgiveness is both an act and a process. That's why the steps given in this chapter may have to be repeated many times. The principles listed will not necessarily be applied in the order given here. But they *must* be applied in order to gain emotional and spiritual healing. These principles of forgiveness have helped me to let go of the bitterness that I had built up toward my mother.

1. *We must see the offender as human.* When we read about those who mistreat children, it is easy to think of such criminals as belonging to another species—to think of them as "animals" rather than as human beings. Indeed, in one sense man is like an animal. When man lives without God, he lives like an animal. The psalmist Asaph wrote of forgetting to look at life from God's viewpoint: "I was as a beast before thee." Indeed, a man left to his own devices is actually worse than an animal because man is clever and creative in his cruelty. No beast is as vindictive, crafty, and debased as a man who dethrones God and pursues his own lustful desires.

But it is important to remember that man is different from animals. All of us are born with a sense of right and wrong. We have the capacity to know God, and we already have eternity planted in our hearts. Man has always had a choice before him: he can either develop his relationship with God or he can pursue sin. Even though the Fall plunged us all into sin, we each have a remnant of the image of God within us.

What distinguishes one human being from another? Only the grace of God and the environment in which he is reared. Thus, it is quite accurate to say that every one of us is innately capable of committing the greatest sin imaginable. The seeds of indescribable evil lie within us all.

Men remain moral beings even after they become criminals. The image of God in man is never completely obliterated, even from the life of the most hardened criminal. That is why most criminals are unable to face themselves. On the one hand they feel compelled to fulfill their evil desires; on the other hand they know intuitively that they are doing wrong. In order to live with themselves they have only one recourse: denial. Needless to say, such individuals develop a hard heart. Paul describes the wicked as being "past feeling." That is, they are incapable of human sympathy and kindness. They have feelings only for themselves. Yet they are still aware of right and wrong at some level.

Imagine what a private hell an abuser must go through when he or she puts to death all natural feelings of compassion. It is not easy to suffocate the natural love that a woman has for her infant, but it can be done. It is not easy to erase the natural affection that a father has toward his children, but it can be squelched if the children interfere with his active pursuit of his own lusts. Every time an individual turns a deaf ear to his conscience and follows his perverted desires, it becomes easier and easier to repeat that behavior. Eventually there is no feeling left.

Thus we must regard the abuser himself as a victim—a victim of his own lusts, bound by selfish desires and hostility. If we knew the truth about such people, if we knew what abuse they had endured, if we understood their apparent helplessness to cope with the pressures of life—then our anger could more easily turn to sympathy.

I know very little about my mother's background or the internal frustrations that she must have felt as she tried to rear my sister and me without a husband and without friends who cared. But I suspect that if I could have uncovered what lay beneath that harsh, uncaring exterior, I would have found a mother who had become a victim of her own hostility, a mother who herself had not received the tender love that everyone craves.

I am not saying that people are not responsible for what they do. Abusers of every stripe are indeed to be held accountable. They can seek help. They can turn to God and others for help. My point is simply that such people often cannot change on their own. And if they refuse to admit their need to others (especially to God), they feel trapped by their own passions and selfish, emotional needs.

In light of that we must ask, How can we expect a young woman to forgive a father for raping her, knowing that he will never be called to account for his crime? Something within each of us screams for justice.

2. *We can forgive without surrendering our desire for justice*. The Bible expressly teaches that we are not to "even the score." Paul wrote, "Never take your own revenge, beloved, but leave room for the wrath of God, for it is written, 'Vengeance is mine, I will repay,' says the Lord" (Romans 12:19).

The person who is willing to forgive without taking vengeance into his own hands must surrender the past to God, the Judge of the universe. We must be willing to believe that God will bring to justice every event that has ever happened. In this perverted world it is necessary to remind ourselves that every court case tried on earth will be reopened. Every act, word, and deed is being accurately recorded for a future accounting. Before God, there will be no recourse to defense attorneys, no legal loopholes, no plea bargaining. There will be only facts—undiluted and undistorted. No one will escape. God will replay it all in slow motion.

His justice will be fully satisfied. Those who accept Christ as Savior receive His mercy, for God's demands were fully paid by Christ; those who do not accept Him will have no one to pay for their sins. Because they can never do so themselves, they will remain eternally guilty and live in hell forever.

Thankfully, because of Christ's death on the cross, those of us who have believed in Him will be spared the wrath of God that we richly deserve. Our lives will also be evaluated, with the purpose of determining what rewards we shall receive in heaven. But the judgment of hell has been borne for us by Christ, our Savior.

Christ was able to endure injustice without needing to settle the score immediately. "And while being reviled, He did not revile in return; while suffering, He uttered no threats, but kept entrusting Himself to Him who judges righteously" (1 Peter 2:23). That helps us understand why the young woman who was raped by her father and brothers can forgive them. She can do that, knowing that some day they shall stand before God and give a full account of their actions. Then God will specify their punishment. Every deed will be accounted for, and justice will be served. God will judge righteously.

Thus we can leave justice to God. He will take care of it for us, as He did for Christ, who refused to retaliate but committed Himself instead to the Father. We can forgive, knowing that our desire for justice will eventually be fully satisfied.

3. *Forgiveness is not an emotion but an act of the will.* We can choose to forgive, whether we feel like it or not.

The desire for revenge is so deeply ingrained in human nature that we find it hard to lay aside our bitterness. To release our feelings to God and let Him take up our cause seems impractical. The fact that so much of our life was ruined because of the abuse we received is difficult to accept, and it is rare to "feel" like forgiving those who have hurt us.

We can say, however, "In the name of Christ I choose to forgive!" even when every fiber of our being resists. Because God commands forgiveness, we must forgive. *He will give us the grace to do what He commands.*

Since anger and bitterness are inwardly destructive, we must acknowledge forgiveness as something good we do for ourselves. I asked one person who came to me for counsel, "Why should your abuser continue to ruin your life? Hasn't he done enough damage to your soul?" If you do not forgive, you are the loser. The offender does not care about you.

Why let him or her continue to control you by harboring feelings that will inhibit your spiritual development?

Give your feelings to God. Give your future to God. You will be surprised at the healing that takes place when God begins to carry your hurts. "Casting all your anxiety upon Him, because He cares for you" (1 Peter 5:7).

4. *Forgiveness is not a one-time act but a process.* Don't be discouraged if you try to forgive only to discover that the bitterness returns. There have been times that I have forgiven someone, and then my feelings of bitterness erupted again later.

Many people find it helpful to write a letter to their abuser without ever mailing it. Or write a letter to a friend describing what happened to you; tell someone who can help bear your pain. The young woman whose story I quoted above said that the letter she wrote me was the first time she had shared her past with anyone. Imagine the torturous pain of bearing those scars within her soul all alone.

Victims of abuse will understand the power of an experience to trigger bitterness that has already been forgiven and (almost) forgotten. Seeing a mother tenderly care for her child can trigger anger toward parents who didn't care for you. Certain rooms or colors can remind you of the abuse suffered in similar surroundings. But do not be discouraged. As you continue to affirm your decision to forgive your abuser, you will find that the bitterness of the past gradually loses its grip. When it reenters your soul, it will not hold as much power over you, nor does it last as long as before.

Like David, there must be a time when we pour out our soul to God. Do this as often as you have to. I have found this to be most helpful in dealing with my own past. I have learned that God has big shoulders; He is able to take the full weight of all our emotional aches and pains.

The young woman whose story began this chapter has little choice but to forgive her cruel, perverted father and brothers. The alternative is to be driven by bitterness and the compulsion for revenge. Such feelings will only prolong the fragmentation that has already occurred in her emotional and spiritual makeup. I pray she will forgive. Thankfully, God is able to help her.

I will extol Thee, O Lord, for Thou has lifted me up,
And hast not let my enemies rejoice over me.
O Lord my God,
I cried to Thee for help, and Thou didst heal me.
O Lord, Thou hast brought up my soul from Sheol;
Thou has kept me alive, that I should not go down to the pit.
Sing praise to the Lord, you His godly ones,
And give thanks to His holy name.
For His anger is but for a moment,
His favor is for a lifetime;
Weeping may last for the night,
But a shout of joy comes in the morning.

(Psalm 30:1-5)

Dear Dorie:

Dorie, when I heard you tell your story, I was so angry. I wondered how anyone could love a God like that! But through your witness and the encouragement of friends, I began to change. During the last two years God broke me and changed my view of Him. I'm still having trouble with my emotions, but I'm not trying to commit suicide anymore as I once did. I've decided to take care of my past and keep following Him!

Love,
S.

7
The Power of the Father's Love

Listen to the cry of a sixteen-year-old whose parents were divorced when she was nine. A few days later her mother married, but shortly thereafter she died. So the girl went to live with her real father, who abused her. Then she was separated from her brothers and sisters and put in a foster home. She speaks for many of us when she writes:

> I've heard of God, but I wonder if He cares. I hated Him when I was growing up. I hated Him for letting me go through what I did. I figured if He loved me, why did He let all this happen? I didn't do anything to deserve this. I was so hurt I started hanging around with other kids who smoked and drank and took pills. I even tried to kill myself.
>
> I've been told I should accept Christ, and I want to, but it's hard to do. Why didn't He help me when I was growing up?
>
> I read your book *Dorie*, and I loved it. I started crying because you are just like me. If you can change, I can too, but it's not easy. If you could help me, I would love it.
>
> Your friend,
> S.

If it is true that we derive our concept of God from our earthly fathers, what hope is there for those of us who were rejected by our fathers and in some cases harshly betrayed? Our heavenly Father did not intervene on our behalf—He actually allows children to be abused to the point of death. That is surely one of the most difficult theological problems we will ever have to resolve. Yet unless we are at peace with our heavenly Father, we will never experience emotional wholeness.

The Pain of Rejection

When my sister and I were growing up in our dingy apartment in Oakland, California, my father visited us only once or twice. After we moved into the orphanage I often thought about him, wondering whether he cared that he had two daughters growing up in the world somewhere. I wondered what it would be like to have a father who cared.

At nineteen I went to considerable trouble to find my father, who was living in Oklahoma. I stayed with him and his wife for about a year and a half and then returned to Oakland to work.

A year later I decided to return to Tulsa to deliver a message to him in person: I wanted him to know that God was calling me to be a missionary. Even though he did not share my love for God, I thought he would be proud of the decision I had made.

After the long train ride, I caught a taxi to his house. I paid the driver and quickly jumped out with my suitcase in hand. My dad was sitting on the porch where he often relaxed.

"Dad!"

"Hi, honey."

I knew that my father was not well. He was suffering from a heart condition and seemed to be in discomfort. "Dorie," he said slowly, "all my life I've had a philosophy to live by. But you know—" He paused, groping for the right words. "You know, now I don't have a philosophy to die by. And I am dying."

This was a moment I had waited for. I shared once again what Christ had done in my life, and I told him that He could prepare anyone for death.

"No! I didn't want Him when I was healthy, and I don't want Him now."

I could scarcely believe my ears, but I had to go on and tell him why I had come. "Dad, I have come to tell you something. God has called me to be a missionary in New Guinea to tell others about Christ. I hope to go to Bible school this fall."

Sick as he was, he stood up from his rocker and turned to face the back of the porch. "If that's what you plan to do, then don't unpack your suitcase. Call a cab now to pick you up. From this moment on, you are not my daughter."

"Dad, you don't mean it!"

"Yes, I do. I never want to see you again."

Tears came to my eyes, but I forced them back. The finality in my father's voice scared me. There was nothing I could say. I went into the house to call a cab, hoping that my father would change his mind. When I returned to the porch he was still standing with his back to me. I tried to hug him, but he stiffened. "Dad, I still love you."

He did not reply. Nor would he turn around. Moments later a cab pulled up in front of the house. I grabbed my suitcase and got into the back seat. As the car pulled away, all I could see was my father's back. That was the last time I saw my father alive.

Rain splashed against the windows of the train as it pulled out of Tulsa for the long trip back to California. Every chug of the steam engine seemed to say, *You're all alone—you're all alone—you're all alone*. I wept openly, fumbling with the moist handkerchief in my hands. For a moment I thought I really was all alone. I had prayed to God about this trip. I had often prayed for my father, but now he had rejected me.

An hour went by before I had the presence of mind to remember that God had not left me. I began to remember some of the passages of Scripture I had memorized years ago. God would be with me. My mother regretted that she had ever borne me. My father had been unconcerned about me in my formative years, and now he had disowned me. I had only one friend—Jesus Christ.

Years later, after I was married, I happened to learn of the death of my father through some friends. Lloyd and I found out as we were returning from a conference in Toronto. We decided to drive to Oklahoma for the wake, which was scheduled for the next day. The funeral was a day later.

When we arrived at the funeral home, I signed my name in the guest book under the heading "Daughters." The funeral director said, "He didn't have any children."

"Oh, yes, I'm his daughter."

"The family is very upset—I don't think you should go in right now."

"We'll come back later when no one is here."

My father was true to his word. His death notice said, "He had no children." The funeral director wanted to respect my father's wishes.

That evening Lloyd and I drove to the funeral home to see my father. "Lloyd, I'm sorry that this is the way you have to meet," I said.

"That's OK. I understand."

My father lay dressed in a dark red robe, his hands folded across his chest. Even in death he was handsome, with his rugged features and dark complexion.

The emotions of many years poured out. "Dad, I loved you! I loved you!" As we turned away, the last words my dad had said to me throbbed in my ears, "I never want to see you again. You are no longer my daughter."

To my knowledge my father rejected Christ's forgiveness to the very end. If so, he and I shall never meet again. The conversation on the front porch was our last; there will not be another good-bye or another hello—ever.

The Search for a Father's Love

Although my father rejected me, he did not abuse me physically. I have discovered that I am quite fortunate when compared to the many people whose fathers inflicted physical and sexual abuse upon them.

A young woman whose mother married an abuser said this of her stepdad, "Between the ages of 8 and 10 I was sexually molested by my stepdad two or three times a week. When I became a teenager the mental anguish was unbearable. I wondered if I would turn out 'gay' or ever be a wife who was really able to satisfy her husband." She goes on to explain that her self-image was further damaged by the remarks he made to her. On the one hand he would say that she would be "beauty queen material" if he could beat her into shape. Then he would say that she was too fat or too ugly to get a boyfriend.

The most common form of sexual abuse is incest between a father and his daughter. It begins with the father's fondling the child, often when the little girl is in bed—the very place that supposedly represents safety and security. The adult in whom she has trusted tells her, "This is what all daddies do to their daughters to show they love them." From there it may progress to other forms of touching and eventually to sexual intercourse.

It is the ultimate form of betrayal. A little girl's daddy is supposed to protect her, but instead he violates her personhood. He is the man whom she most trusted, the one whom she admired, but he uses the private parts of her body for his own gratification. He warns her not to tell anyone, for it is their secret. In some instances the father will actually threaten the child, saying that if she tells her mother he will deny it. Everyone will just think the girl is a liar, he says.

At breakfast he treats her as if nothing happened. All day long the girl thinks about what happened the night before, but she cannot put the pieces of the puzzle in place. How could her father, who claims to love her, have done this to her?

The overpowering personality of her father makes it almost impossible for the child to resist him or tell another adult. She fears her father's warnings; she also feels shame, which keeps her locked inside her own prison.

In some instances the child may come to physically enjoy the sexual stimulation. This only adds to the guilt she feels. She thinks others can see her mind and heart; therefore she becomes withdrawn.

For the rest of her life, this woman searches for a "father" she can trust. But where can she find one? Her earthly protector victimized her; could not her heavenly Protector do the same?

The problem goes even deeper. God, her heavenly Father, stood by, watching what happened and apparently did nothing. How can He claim to love the world if He is silent when children are abused? Her earthly father abused her, while her heavenly Father neglected her.

Adopted into Another Family

Virtually all abused children question the love of God. Most feel anger toward Him. Unless they overcome their bitterness toward the Almighty, they cannot experience emotional healing and put the past behind them. How can an abused child develop a healthy relationship with God?

As I have already mentioned, we must begin by accepting Christ as our Savior. This is the first step and the most important. All of us have sinned, and we can only be part of God's family by accepting the gift of forgiveness and eternal life. Remember that Christ's death on the cross was a sacrifice for sin—a payment that allows God to forgive us and welcome us into His family. This gift must be received by faith. Once we receive it, we become children of the most high God. When I accepted Christ on that chair in the orphanage, I began a relationship with God that continues until this day.

Second, we must accept God's plan, even though we cannot understand it. I am the first to admit that I do not know why God allows atrocities to go on in this world without intervening. But I do know that God loves me more than any earthly father could.

I am comforted in the midst of this confusion when I think of the cross. God did not protect His own Son from the wounds of wicked men. The One who was sinless endured abuse, though ten thousand angels were sitting in the wings ready to rescue Him. Because He allowed that act of cruelty, healing can flow to the world. I have to believe that is the reason God does not intervene today: He wants to show His power to bring good out of evil and His grace in the midst of human brutality and sin.

I know that God's agenda is different from mine. He has chosen not to give us all the answers. But He has promised that He will bless us if we believe that He knows best. That means that we must submit to God's authority without bitterness. How much better to experience the warmth of His love than to drift angrily away from His healing grace!

We must "forgive" God for what happened to us. Of course, God does not really need our forgiveness. He has done nothing wrong. But we must pour out our souls to Him and tell Him when we doubt His love and find His ways confusing. We must be willing to give Him our bitterness. He honors honesty.

Let me pause here and say that for many people such communication is a process that continues over a long period of time. Loving God is an act of the will, but it is also an attitude that takes time to develop.

Communication with the Father

God can handle our anger, our guilt, and our deepest hurts. Read the psalms, and you will see David admitting his doubts and expressing disappointment with God. In Psalm 77:7-9 the poet Asaph expresses his frustration with the Almighty:

> Will the Lord reject forever? And will He be favorable again? Has His lovingkindness ceased forever? Has His promise come to an end forever? Has God forgotten to be gracious? Or has He in anger withdrawn His compassion?

God brought him through that bitter experience, and by the end of the psalm he was giving thanks to God for His faithfulness. God can dissolve our disappointments and doubts. If you are angry with God, share your feelings reverently but honestly. He will understand. Then He will give you promises to assure you that He loves you and cares.

Let me conclude this chapter with another letter. It is from a woman who read my previous book. She had been in foster homes, detentions, and jails since the age of three. Her mother died of an overdose of heroin, and she saw her father only once, when she was fifteen. He also was using the needle. Today this young woman is living with a fine Christian woman who is helping her through her fourth pregnancy. Her first child was given up for adoption; her second had to be taken away at the age of six months; the third was aborted.

She writes that she has been in the drug, alcohol, sex, and gang scene, but she wants to change. But like anyone who has been abused, she struggles with accepting the love of God because of the deep hurts her own parents inflicted upon her. She was in a mood to communicate to her father, so she wrote:

> Dorie, I was thinking about my earthly father, and I was wondering what it would be like to write to him. Then I was thinking how he left me and didn't love me. Then I began to think about my heavenly Father who was always there when I needed Him, but I've been blind to His love and deaf to His word. But most of all I have been stubborn. So I decided to write Him a letter instead.
>
> > O dear Father:
> >
> > I'm so sorry I've hurt You and rejected You so many times. Why couldn't I just come to my senses and realize that You love me and always did—even when I was just a little kid. You always loved me and still do, but I just kept on hurting You.
> >
> > O dear Father, I'm so sorry for the tears I caused You to cry. But now I am so happy . . . for You died for my tears. Thank You that because of Jesus You are my Father.
> >
> > Sunshine

God can replace the gloom with sunshine and the rebellion with feelings of acceptance. There is power in the Father's forgiveness, strength in the Father's love, and assurance in the Father's care. We can each adopt the name "Sonshine," for His Son shines in our hearts. "My father and my mother have forsaken me, but the Lord will take me up" (Psalm 27:10).

Dear Dorie:

Dorie, I've talked to people about the problems I'm having in my family, but they don't understand the hurts, the loneliness that I feel, because they've not been there. That's why it helped so much to talk to you. Satan knew your words would help me win the battle against my feelings. I'm going to fight this warfare with the Lord's help, and I know we will win. What makes me want to keep fighting is that I want to be someone! I want to help those who are hurting like you have. I'm so excited for my future, which I used to dread. I thought that the future would hold more hurts from my family, but, praise God, He is using those hurts to help me reach out and help others. Now I am willing to hurt if it helps me to know the hurts of others.

Love,
B.

8
The Power of Christ over Satan

A young woman came up to me when I was speaking to a group of people in Canada. "If I could, I would smash you in the face!" she said, standing before me with a clenched fist. She looked as if she might follow through with her threat. But she could not—at least she did not move her arm forward. I believe the Lord was holding her back and was glad that several people stood by to restrain her.

I walked over to her as she lashed out in bitterness and anger. "It doesn't matter what you say," I told her. "God still loves you." Later I was told that she began pounding the pews with her fists and kicking those who were trying to help her.

"Does this happen often when you speak?" asked a reporter who was there to interview me.

"Sometimes," I replied. "When a surgeon hits a raw nerve, it hurts."

And hurt it does.

There is more to that woman's story. She had made some wrong responses to abuse in her past, and she was troubled by evil spirits who used every opportunity to exploit her weaknesses and sins. Fortunately, some individuals at the meeting had some knowledge of spiritual warfare and had the ability to confront such wicked powers with the authority of Christ.

I've often wished that we only had to cope with our own emotional and spiritual bruises. But the fact remains that Satan is behind many of our battles, and his chief delight is to take a difficult situation and make it worse. The ruler of this world wants to destroy us, impede our emotional healing, and keep us in bondage. He contests every step we take toward inner healing.

What Satan Can Do

Satan is not omnipresent, that is, he cannot be everywhere at the same time. In fact, he cannot even be two places at once. But he is able to travel from one end of the earth to the other in a split second. He also has tens of thousands of demons to do his bidding and work with him to destroy us.

Satan has been given authority to rule this world. One day he showed Christ the kingdoms of this world and said, "I will give You all this domain and its glory; for it has been handed over to me, and I give it to whomever I wish" (Luke 4:6). Christ did not contradict this stupendous claim. Just think, Satan had the power to give Christ the whole earth if only the Lord would worship him! High on that mountain Christ and Satan could look over the evil one's domain. Of course Christ did not take him up on his offer, but Satan apparently had every right to make it.

Satan and his underlings are able to attach themselves to people, houses, and even animals (cf. Mark 5:13). Once such an attachment is made they do their best to cling to that entity and to exert control over it. Above all they desire power and the total corruption of that which is good. How do they gain an advantage over human beings, particularly children who have been abused?

Satan's influence begins with the abuser himself. There is no other way to explain how a mother can attempt to drown her daughter in a bathtub, except to recognize the power of cruel demons who seek to torment and destroy human beings. How else can one explain a father's warped desires that cause him to sexually molest his little girl? Whatever human factors contribute to such perversions, they are intensified by evil spirits. Thus a child who grows up in an abusive home may already be in an environment that is conducive to the influence of evil spirits. The sins of the fathers are often visited upon the children to the fourth generation. Thankfully, this cycle can be broken.

Wicked spirits can also exploit a trauma situation, quite apart from the influence of the family itself. They have access to the human mind. Any fears, anger, and bitterness can become inroads for agitation and demonic involvement. Paul taught that if we let the sun go down upon our anger, we are giving the devil a foothold (Ephesians 4:26-27). The longer such negative emotions fester, the more likely they are to become demonic footholds.

A third way Satan gains his advantage is through unconfessed sin or willful disobedience. Immorality, involvement in occultic practices, and the viewing of movies with sexual, violent, or demonic themes all provide an entry for Satan and his cohorts to do his work. *Evil spirits work through the sins of the flesh to accomplish their objectives.* The spirits exploit the evil that is already present by making it attractive and addictive. In that way Satan can do his most powerful work and remain completely hidden.

Therefore we must learn to rebuke Satan even when we cannot see open evidence of his power. He is often working through guilt, anger, or emotional instability. We can be quite certain that Satan and his demons have at least some involvement with psychological and emotional disorders of all kinds, even if we cannot always pinpoint their activity. Some cases are rather obvious; others are not.

How We Can Resist Satan

How do we combat his influence? Following are some steps that will lead to freedom from Satan's power—steps that will thwart his attempts to keep us hostage to our past.

First we must yield ourselves wholly to God. We must give everything to Christ, including our scars. Please don't think this is easy to do. By nature we want to hold onto our hurts because we think we have a right to them. After all, if we give them to Christ, we will no longer have a legitimate reason to feel sorry for ourselves!

How vividly I recall my own struggles, especially as I began to give my scars to Christ. To give Him my future and my marriage and my children was easy, for I delighted to give Him the ones whom I loved. But to give Him those hurts, to let go of my bitterness—that was more difficult. Thankfully, He gave me the grace to do it.

As believers we already belong to Christ, for our body is His temple (1 Corinthians 6:19-20). Submission is simply acknowledging that Christ is our rightful owner. This continuous act on our part causes the power of Satan to be diminished. Specifically James wrote, "Submit therefore to God. Resist the devil and he will flee from you" (James 4:7).

That is not to say that Satan will immediately leave us. When Christ was in the desert, He quoted Scripture and told the enemy to flee. But Satan immediately returned with another temptation. In fact, Luke reports, "And when the devil had finished every temptation, he departed from Him until an opportune time" (Luke 4:13). He has a way of finding those "opportune times."

Submission must therefore be a repeated experience for each of us. It includes giving Christ all of our bruises, our feelings of anger and revenge, and our nightmares and flashbacks. It means giving Him *everything*.

Second, we must understand that Satan and his demons have already been defeated. The cross won a decisive and permanent victory over the forces of evil. "When He had disarmed the rulers and authorities, He made a public display of them, having triumphed over them through Him" (Colossians 2:15). We do not battle Satan from a position of weakness but from a position of strength.

Third, and most important, we must learn that we are completely and unconditionally accepted by Christ. We are no longer alone in our struggles, so we must not continue to focus on our failures and defeats. The name of every one of His children is on God's list of valuables. We are important to God Himself!

Satan strikes at our self-worth, at our value as individuals. He wants us to feel dirty, guilty, hopeless, and unloved. People who are demonized are also demoralized; they feel overwhelmed by circumstances and overcome by their own emotional deficiencies. Satan tells us we are the scum of the earth.

In order to learn to view ourselves as conquerors instead of as victims, we must believe what the Bible says about us rather than our own distorted self-perceptions. "For you have not received a spirit of slavery leading to fear again, but you have received a spirit of adoption as sons by which we cry out, 'Abba! Father!' The Spirit Himself bears witness with our spirit that we are children of God . . . if indeed we suffer with Him in order that we may also be glorified with Him" (Romans 8:15-17). God has greatly exalted His own children. We will one day reign with Christ. We will participate in glorious triumph for all eternity.

We must concentrate on all that God has done for us in Christ so that we may lead a life of praise and worship. To offer praise is to glorify God. Nothing causes evil spirits more consternation than our giving thanks to God and developing the discipline of thanksgiving. I love the psalms. They express the depths of human despair but also bring us to the height of human adoration. "I will extol Thee, my God, O King; and I will bless Thy name forever and ever. Every day I will bless Thee, and I will praise Thy name forever and ever. Great is the Lord and highly to be praised; and His greatness is unsearchable" (Psalm 145:1-3). To read such expression of praise is to rebuke the thoughts and suggestions of our soul's enemy. If we make every day a day of praise and thanksgiving, we will find it easier to believe God's Word than Satan's lies.

Good music is abhorrent to the devil as well. Let me encourage you to use a stereo to your maximum advantage. Play recordings of the *Messiah* or praise songs whenever possible. Filling one's mind with triumphant singing will weaken Satan's strongholds.

Finally, we must understand the spiritual armor listed in Ephesians 6 and be certain that we are prepared for the battle. Let us remember that Satan wins many battles, but he is doomed to lose the war.

"Giving thanks to the Father, who has qualified us to share in the inheritance of the saints in light. For He delivered us from the domain of darkness, and transferred us to the kingdom of His beloved Son" (Colossians 1:12-13). In Christ we can trample the enemy. We can become emotionally whole. Thanks to Him there is life after abuse, in spite of Satan.

Dear Dorie:

Dorie, I wanted so desperately to escape out of the meeting, but I couldn't. Dorie, how did you get past that barrier of God's love? I just can't trust, I can't believe. And now, you go on loving and receiving love—that means being vulnerable. Don't you get hurt? Doesn't life teach you that love is false, that people don't really love when you think they do? Where do you get your strength from? Do you understand what I'm saying? Is there an answer? I doubt it.

Love,
E.

9
Someone Is Taking Care of Me

Sexual abuse takes place all over the world. I have always known that, but it becomes more evident to me when I take to other countries the same message of hope that I present in the United States. I'm grateful for the opportunity to travel. Everywhere I go, I have found that people respond to a message of hope. I've also found that God prepared the way for me. His gracious protection has enabled me to witness transformed lives.

I was invited to participate in a wedding during a visit to Romania. The bride was a lovely woman who had served as my interpreter. She had heard me tell my story of childhood trauma and of the difference Christ can make. The day of the wedding she whispered to me, "I want you to know that I had a background similar to yours." She did not have to elaborate.

"I understand," I said as I gently touched her arm.

During the reception I noticed that her father did not look at his lovely daughter; not once did he lift his eyes to see her happy face. She reached over and took my hand. "See what I mean?"

"Yes. I know." I took her hand as the tears rolled down our cheeks. I told her that I hoped that she would be as happy as Lloyd and I had been. I thought of how gentle and understanding he had been during our thirty-six years of marriage. This young woman could also have a happy marriage, if her husband would understand.

In addition to a universal receptiveness to God's message of hope, I have also experienced God's care and concern for me in unique ways during my travels. In fact, I am somewhat hesitant to share the following stories because they are so unusual—or miraculous. Some may find it difficult to believe that they actually happened. But these experiences are a credit to my heavenly Father and confirm His special concern for me, His servant.

This visit to Romania took place before the revolution in late 1989, which toppled the Ceausescu regime. Security was tight and freedom restricted. Mia and Costel Oglice, a Romanian couple on staff at Precept Ministries, had arranged that we meet them there, so that I could share my testimony in various churches. I consider these dear friends my second family and rejoiced in the privilege of ministering with them in Romania.

There I discovered the miraculous power of God's care for me in a time of need. In fact, I believe I may have encountered angels sent by my heavenly Father for my protection and personal help. I want to let those who have been abused know that we are the objects of God's love and care. When we are in trouble, God sometimes does the unexpected. The following experiences are a message of healing and hope. They affirm the truth that God cares for those in need.

An Angel of God

My stay in Romania had come to an end. I was to board a plane and fly to Vienna before returning to the United States. I decided to check out of the hotel several hours before I needed to get to the airport. I wanted to sit in the lobby and watch the people until it was time to catch a cab. I had been there twenty minutes when the secret police appeared, swarming all over the area, blocking the elevators, and telling everyone to leave. I had no idea what the man was trying to say to me until the woman behind the desk shouted in English, "Emergency! Go into the bar!"

"I'm not going into the bar!"

The man shouted the same command again, but I refused to go. *What can they do to me on my last day here?* I thought.

The woman behind the desk finally gave in and said, "Just sit!"

I sat. Of course, I didn't know whether a bomb was expected to explode or the hotel was on fire. But a moment later I met two English-speaking Israelis who explained that their Prime Minister was about to arrive. I breathed a sigh of relief.

The dim chandelier in the lobby was suddenly turned up to full voltage. Several men with carts filled with trinkets scurried across the lobby to put gifts on the shelves of the until then empty gift shop. Within minutes there were decorations in the windows and the semblance of merchandise for sale.

The doors opened and in came the Prime Minister, his wife, and his entourage. The delegates were escorted to the gift shop, where they purchased a few items and then disappeared into the elevator. The doors had scarcely closed when the chandelier was dimmed again and workmen came out of nowhere to put the items in the gift shop back into boxes to store them away.

I was grateful that I had left my room early, for the elevators remained off limits to the hotel guests. But the experience made me want to get to the airport as quickly as possible. So I asked the woman at the desk to get me a cab. "No, it is not time for you to leave yet," she said, obviously aware of the time my plane was scheduled to depart. But I insisted that she get me a cab immediately. I could sit at the airport for several hours just as easily as in the hotel lobby, I reasoned. At last she relented.

At that moment, a tall, handsome man walked through the lobby toward me. The woman spoke to him in the native language and then turned to me and said, "I've asked him to get a cab for you."

The man said to me, "I am here to help you. Will you follow me?" I agreed.

He got a cab, and we both climbed in wordlessly. When we arrived at the airport, hundreds of people swarmed through the entrances. Inside the building itself there was incredible commotion everywhere. In the distance I could see the Israeli plane surrounded by the military.

I looked at the long lines at the customs and immigration stands and wondered if I would ever be able to get through the confusion and required detailed inspections. One man had hidden some silver candlesticks in his suitcase; they were taken from him. He and his wife became angry and wept. For a moment my heart sank. I wasn't even sure where I was to go.

"Don't be concerned. I'm here to help you. Just follow me!" the man repeated with calm confidence. Though I did not tell him my airline (indeed at that moment I couldn't remember which one I was flying), he took me directly to Lufthansa. We came to a long line that appeared to be totally stalled. The wait, I feared, would be interminable. I hesitated, but he said, "No, follow me. Remember, I am here to help you."

He then took me past all the people in line and told me to stand at the head of the line, next to another man. "Thank you. I will," I replied. The man next to me was from England. We shook hands.

"I don't know who is in charge of this mess!" he commented.

"I don't either, sir, but I know who is in charge of me."

"Who's that?"

"The Lord!"

"I'm sticking with you!"

The tall man who had brought me to the airport was still standing by my side. The inspection agent called, "Suitcase!"

I went to grab my suitcase, but he said, "No, don't touch it. I'm here to help you." With that he lifted my suitcase and said to the agent, "Let her through."

"No," was the reply.

"Let her through. She is fine."

"No!"

"Let her through; she's fine—and let this man through also. He's fine, too."

With that, my anonymous friend picked up the Englishman's suitcase and handed it to the official. With a gesture of despair the official sent the suitcases through without opening them.

"Sir, I don't know how to say this to you," I said, looking into the kind eyes of the tall, helpful gentleman, "but God must have sent you to help me."

He looked at me with a loving smile, put his hand on my shoulder, and said, "And may His blessing rest upon you all the days of your life."

The Englishman whispered, "What a kind man to help us like that! I appreciate it. By the way, where is he?"

I turned back toward the kind stranger, but he was gone. Both of us looked around, but he had disappeared from our view. "Sir," I said to the Englishman, "I don't know what you are going to think about this, but I think we just saw an angel!"

"Aw, come on."

We heard the call for our flight, and as I was about to pick up my handbag the Englishman said, "No! I'm helping you!"

We decided to sit together on the plane. I told him some of what God had done in my life. When we arrived at Vienna, he decided to help me through customs. As we parted he clasped my hand and told me how glad he was to have met me. Then just as I was about to leave, he pulled me aside and said, "By the way, Dorie, I think you may have been right!"

The above incident prepared me for a similar one, which occurred a year later, also in Eastern Europe.

Another Angel of God

During Ceausescu's reign, travel even within the country was highly restricted. To go from one city to another I had to obtain special permission and clear inspections. I needed to visit another city within a certain country. When I arrived at customs, I found that several lines of people had formed to go through the inspection. An agent waved me over to his counter. I hesitated because above him was a sign that read "Diplomat." I thought there was some mistake. But when he continued to insist, I thought, *Sure, I'll go. Why not? I'm a diplomat for Christ!*

"Do you have a book?" he asked.

"No, but I have *Reader's Digest*," I said, understanding full well that that was not the Book he meant.

"No. Do you have a book?"

"No."

"Then go through."

When I arrived at my destination, my friends met me in the hotel. I had the privilege of visiting various churches and telling them what God had done for me despite my background. Some people were surprised that I had had such a hard life growing up in the United States. It helped them realize that life can be difficult no matter where one is reared —even in the great United States of America.

When the time came to leave that city, Nickie, a young American woman who was traveling with me, and I had to retrace our steps and return to the city from which we had come. From there we would fly back to the United States. Once again we had to pass through customs inspection. Our travel agency in the United States had given us tickets that were to qualify us to visit several cities, so we expected no difficulty with the flight. However, when we showed our tickets, we were repeatedly told, "No!"

What were we to do?

In desperation I went to another official, a woman who was even more discourteous than the man. Ahead of me someone was trying to get a computer through customs; the agent not only took it out of its case but also partially took it apart.

"Please, may I go through?" I asked.

"No!" was the cold reply.

I tried other officials, frantically trying to find someone who could help us clear inspection. We received the same heartless response from everyone. For twenty minutes we tried to get someone to let us through but to no avail.

Suddenly, a man appeared who spoke English. "Come with me, and I will help you," he said.

I began to tell him what I needed, but he interrupted me. "I know what you need," he said. "I have a cab waiting."

"But what about our suitcases?"

"I'll get them for you." He said something to one of the officials and began taking our belongings out to the curb where the cab was waiting.

Nickie whispered to me, "Dorie! What are you doing? We don't know him!"

"He speaks English, and he's got a cab. Let's go." We got into the cab, and he drove us to the downtown area of the huge city.

"We'll make your flight," he assured us.

We drove up in front of a building, and a moment later a man walked by. "I know him. He is the head of the travel bureau," he said. Then he caught the man's attention, said something in the national language, and the gentleman walked over to the car. In English he said, "Why yes, Mrs. Van Stone, I know all about you. Go over to that building. There is a ticket waiting for you."

Our new friend went into the building with us, and we found the tickets waiting for us. Then we got back into the cab to go to the airport.

"Will we make it?" I asked.

"Oh, sure," he replied. He took us to the second terminal, assuring us once again that we would be able to catch our flight. There was no need for concern, he said. Then he took our suitcases out of the car.

"You may need this," he said, handing us two hundred units of the country's currency. "I'm glad I could be of help," he added. With that he was gone.

We were dumbfounded. In that country no one gave away anything for nothing. What is more, we had not given him any information about our problem at the airport, nor had we told him who we were. Yet he knew our names, the nature of our difficulty, and how to help us. He did not charge us for the cab, and actually gave us two hundred units of the nation's currency.

"Who was he, Dorie?" Nickie gasped.

"I don't know!"

We came to the ticket counter, and the agent said, "Your luggage is overweight. You owe one hundred seventy-five."

I don't have it, I thought—and then remembered, *Of course! The two hundred units are in my pocket.* I gave him the money, and he returned the twenty-five. We got on the plane and were given insipid drinks that did not seem suited to our Western taste buds. Naturally we assumed it was free, but the stewardess came by and said, "Eleven dollars each, please." (Of course she spoke of the national currency.) I gave her the twenty-five, and I received three back. "Lord, You always do everything in abundance!"

And so we arrived at our destination with three units of currency, which was three more than we had had at the beginning of the day!

We told our Christian friends about the incident, and they were just as astounded as we had been. They agreed that there was no human explanation for the incident.

The verse I had claimed for the trip was Psalm 41:1*b*-2, "The Lord will deliver him in a day of trouble. The Lord will protect him, and keep him alive, and he shall be called blessed upon the earth; and do not give him over to the desire of his enemies." He had delivered me through the direct intervention of a gracious man sent to minister to Nickie and me because we were heirs of salvation.

The miracles of that trip were not yet over. The flight I just described was within the country, and I was still scheduled to minister there for several more weeks. I noticed that my passport allowed me to stay only fifteen more days rather than the eight weeks I had planned to stay. The hotel clerk told me to go to the police station to see if I could get an extension. I met two American women who were in essentially the same predicament; they wanted to visit several more cities before going home. So Nickie and I invited them to go to the station with us. At the station the two women were called to the desk first.

"No!" was the rude reply to their request. The women gave further explanation for the request, but the impatient officer refused to listen. I thought certainly I would suffer the same fate. I explained that I needed an extension. He looked at me and replied, "Of course."

He granted the request and added, "Have a nice time."

The difference was so striking that it could not have been coincidence. I always knew that God is able to give us favor even among unbelievers when we are on a mission for Him. That was simply another example of how the Lord took care of us, His people.

I don't know why God has done so many special things for me. They are special reminders, bonuses that God gives over and above His regular blessings. It is His way of saying, "I love you and I care." No matter where I go I've learned that I am not alone

Dear Dorie:

Until I heard you speak I didn't realize how much bitterness there was toward my mother who had abused me. For the first time, I really saw the hurt in my life and realized that I had to lift my mind and soul to God to be cleansed. At the luncheon, a burden was lifted from my heart and shoulders. I praise God for sending you to me. I know Satan will work in my life, but with God's help I will conquer.

Love,
S.

10
Only One Life to Live

I'm impressed by the fact that we each have only a specific number of years to live before we see our Savior and give an account to Him for what we have done on this earth. How quickly life hurries on to its appointed end.

Recently on a flight over California I gazed out of the window of the plane and saw a blur of green far beneath me. Spring was on its way, but it had not yet come into its fullness. Soon the brown earth would give way to the green foliage of trees and plants. Life would break forth. I thought of how often I used to long for heaven, weary of days filled with busy schedules and nights of loneliness. Yet the Lord seemed to say, "I have a plan for you, a plan that includes your life, your heartaches, and your ministry."

"But Lord, I want to be with You," I would whisper. "I long to be in Your presence. Mine is not a death wish—just a growing desire to be with You." I knew that my darling daughter would say, "No, Mom, we need you!" My son would say, "Mother, we need you as we seek for direction in our lives."

Thirty thousand feet above the earth that day I composed a letter to God:

"Lord, I look down and see the winding river moving slowly. On either side there is lush greenery that has been nourished by the water. I want to be like that—providing nutrients that will help people grow, giving them a reason to bloom for you.

"I also know that there are rocks in that river, but it is those obstacles that give the river its sound and its song. Just so, I want to let the Holy Spirit flow through my life to bless everyone I touch. I want to bring a bit of music to some struggling hearts.

"Lord, that river is cleansed as it flows along, taking the debris out of the way. Take all the clutter out of my own life so that my witness will be clear and my life a credit to Your cleansing grace.

"Lord, I felt depressed yesterday, so tired, so undone—it would have been wonderful to slip away into Your presence. But today I am refreshed, willing once again to fulfill the plan You have for me on this earth.

"I know it's not what *I* can do, but what *we* can do. With You I can rise up with wings like an eagle. I can run and not be weary; I can walk and not faint. Thank you for the promise 'For the Lord of hosts has planned, and who can frustrate it?'

"The captain has just told us that we are . . . to land in 20 minutes. We are requested to fasten our seat belts and put our trays in the upright position. . . . Thank you, Lord, for sitting next to me and giving us a safe landing. Some day I will land on that blessed shore, and I know that You and my dear husband, along with many friends, will be waiting as the plane comes to the gate.

"But [for] that day [I] must still wait a while. As for now You seem to be saying, 'Let Me take your hand, and let's go.'"

I got off the plane, realizing that the same Lord whom I had met in the orphanage would continue to hold my hand

and lead me along life's painful journey. And He would graciously use me to touch others' lives as well.

In Toronto there is an organization that helps women with special needs readjust to life. They have been abused, thrown out of their homes, or recently divorced. One of the requirements is that each woman read my previous book, *Dorie: The Girl Nobody Loved*, and write a report on it.

On a recent speaking engagement in Toronto I was given the report written by one woman. She clearly states the purpose of my life, and the report is indeed a fitting summary of all that God has done for me.

The woman writes that throughout my book she saw spiritual growth. "Dorie began in the blackest depths of life but emerges, holding God's hand in victory." She suggests that the title of the book is misleading because "Dorie *was* loved and felt love from the most important person ever—God. She felt His love more strongly than many who come from good homes."

"I think," she continues, "it hinges on the metaphor of the diamond against the black backdrop. Against a white backdrop the splendor of the diamond is not as easily seen. The black backdrop does not change the value of the diamond, but only increases its brilliance and clarity."

She emphasized the fact that we can truly feel God's love best when it is the only thing we have. "We can really hear God's voice when it is the only voice that reaches out and touches us.

"God saved Dorie from the deep emotional scars that she . . . had from the awful and traumatic experience of her childhood. She truly was saved from hell—the hell of trying to cope with these problems alone. Hell comes when there is no one there to listen, no one who feels our pain.

"Dorie's life did not get better after trusting the Lord, but harder. She went from mental to physical abuse. Her suffering was intense, but so was her love for the Lord. She put her hand in God's hand and when it got tough she squeezed harder.

"When she became older she had the freedom to do the will of God. Then the blessings started to come. It was payback time!

"When things got better she didn't forget where she came from but remained faithful to the Lord. She endured much out on the mission field and didn't adopt the attitude that since she had already suffered, how dare God ask her to sacrifice now. She depended on Him in the difficult times and praised Him when things went well."

The woman admits that the book was difficult to read because it brought to mind her own painful past. Whereas I had opened my heart to the Lord at a young age, this woman said that her own heart had been closed during her difficult days—so closed that she "could not hear His knock." She went through the pain and hurt alone. "But that was then and this is now," she concludes. "The fight will not be easy, but if Dorie can do it, so can I."

Yes, she can! With God's help we all can make it.

I can honestly say that there is nothing in my life I would change. Not because all my scars have healed or because my hatred of abuse has dissipated, because neither has happened. But I can say I wouldn't change anything for this one reason: God has been glorified through my suffering. And He has used me to give hope to others whose scars are as bad or even worse than mine.

Years after my story was first written I met with Irma Freman, the Christian matron who gave me a copy of the New Testament just before I left the orphanage. She told me that she had thought about adopting me at that time, but single women were not allowed to do so. It would have been too discouraging for me to know that before I left the orphanage. Someone had actually loved me and cared about me!

I'm glad that I didn't know Irma wanted to adopt me, until after I had gone through all that suffering in foster homes. God did not want me to know that bit of information until I had weathered those storms. God wanted to prove that He can take care of a dirty, unwanted child. He could help me endure the beatings, the sexual abuse, and the rejection from my father as well as from my mother. God wanted to prove a point, and He did. Now I have the privilege of telling thousands of people that God can take "nobodys" and make them into "somebodys" for His name's sake.

> I waited patiently for the Lord; and He inclined to me, and heard my cry. He brought me up out of the pit of destruction, out of the miry clay; and He set my feet upon a rock making my footsteps firm. And He put a new song in my mouth, a song of praise to our God; many will see and fear, and will trust in the Lord. (Psalm 40:1-3)

With His help I want to be faithful until my plane lands and I see my Savior at the gate. The foster homes of my childhood and the disappointments of later years will soon vanish when I move into my permanent residence.

Face to face I'll worship the One who came to me in the orphanage and said, "I love you." And everything will be all right.

Moody Press, a ministry of the Moody Bible Institute,
is designed for education, evangelization, and edification.
If we may assist you in knowing more about Christ
and the Christian life, please write us without obligation:
Moody Press, c/o MLM, Chicago, Illinois 60610.